KT-385-656

SOUPS

Introduction

There are times when only a steaming bowl of hot soup will do… Our Soup book offers more than 60 recipes that everyone can make, and they're good for you too. Whether you like comforting creamy soups, nourishing broths, or something spicier, we've got soup covered.

Every recipe has been triple-tested to ensure perfect results, and if you should find yourself missing that all-important piece of cookware, visit the home of creative kitchenware at www.lakeland.co.uk. You're sure to find just what you're looking for, from dependable basics such as foil and baking parchment, to equipment that will serve you well through many years of cookery to come.

LAKELAND

Lakeland and ACP Magazines Ltd hereby exclude all liability to the extent permitted by law for any errors or omissions in this book and for any loss, damage or expense (whether direct or indirect) suffered by a third party relying on any information contained in this book.

This book was created for Lakeland by ACP Books
Copyright © ACP Magazines Ltd 2009

All rights reserved. No part of this publication may be reproduced, stored in a retrieval system or transmitted by any means, electronic, mechanical, photocopying, recording or otherwise without the prior permission of the copyright holder.

ISBN: 978-1-903777-61-9

Printed and bound in China

contents

tips & techniques

making good soups great

Since Neolithic times, soup has been known to possess restorative and nourishing qualities – the aged and infirm were kept alive by being fed simple meat broths. This concept may have developed over the aeons, but we can all probably remember our mother perched on the edge of our sickbed, urging us to eat a bowl of chicken broth because 'it'll make you feel better'.

Soup can be quickly made from a few inexpensive ingredients, and recent studies show that prefacing a meal with a low-fat soup can help with weight loss by decreasing appetite for the following courses.

Soups form a staple food group in any cuisine, and are all improved if based on homemade stock (see recipes on pages 6 to 7). But the convenience, ease and speed of preparation afforded by the use of packaged stocks, stock cubes and powder can't be denied. Use the best quality prepared stock bases you can find, but bear in mind that they can be very salty and/or full of calories.

homemade stock tips

Any of our basic stock recipes (pages 6 to 7) can take on Mediterranean or Asian flavours with a bit of ingenuity. Add fresh herbs shortly before the stock is ready, and dry-fry spices separately, until just fragrant, before adding to the basic stock ingredients at the start of preparation.

- Chopped chilli, fish sauce and lemongrass impart the taste of Thai seasonings.
- Torn fresh oregano or basil leaves and crushed garlic cloves convert stock into an Italian soup base (try adding a tablespoon of pesto as an alternative).
- Cumin, preserved lemon, cinnamon and a teaspoon of harissa are redolent of Moroccan dishes.
- Add chopped parsley, some olive oil, lemon juice and a dash of allspice to echo the taste of the Middle East.

Other tips for homemade stock include:

■ Clarify stock by stirring 1 lightly beaten egg white and 1 cracked eggshell per litre of stock into a pot of fairly cool stock. Return pot to low heat; slowly return stock to a simmer, without stirring. Simmer 15 minutes, ignoring frothy scum that appears on surface of stock. Take stockpot off heat; cool for about 30 minutes. Using a ladle, push scum aside; scoop stock into muslin-lined sieve placed over a large bowl. Refrigerate until you're ready to freeze or use the stock.

■ Before freezing stock, refrigerate until cold. Carefully scoop off the fat that rises to the top of stock and discard it.

■ If you want to use stock immediately, blot the surface with a few sheets of absorbent paper.

■ Freeze the degreased cooled stock in useful quantities. It can be frozen in empty, cleaned milk cartons; fill to about 3cm from the top of container, cover with a small plastic bag and stand upright in the freezer. Once frozen, seal the carton using masking tape or rubber bands, and stack cartons on their sides in freezer. You can also freeze stock in ice-cube trays; once frozen solid, place cubes in a sealable plastic bag and use singly or as required.

thickening soups

■ Simmer the soup, uncovered, until it cooks down to the desired thickness. Or purée some of the soup's solids then return them to the pan to thicken the broth.

■ Spoon a little of the hot broth into a small bowl, cool it for 5 minutes, then whisk in a few tablespoons of plain flour; once the flour mixture is smooth, stir it into the simmering soup.

■ Cornflour or arrowroot can be blended with a little cold water and stirred into simmering soup.

■ Grate a raw potato into the simmering soup and stir until it is cooked and the soup has thickened.

■ Beat a few of the egg yolks leftover from when you clarified the stock into a little of the hot broth in a separate small bowl, then whisk this mixture into the hot soup.

■ Cream, yogurt, soured cream, crème fraîche and even grated cheese can all be used to thicken soups. Stabilise the chosen dairy product first by blending it with a little cornflour then whisking some of the hot stock into the mixture before adding to the soup

serving containers and garnishes

■ A soup tureen and ladle make a spectacular way of presenting a main course soup at a special meal.

■ If you can, choose serving bowls to suit the soup (rice bowls for Oriental soups, earthenware bowls for heavier soups, and so on). If in doubt, use a large flat soup bowl – they are easy to eat from and garnished soup looks fantastic in them.

Possibilities for garnishes include:

■ For thick soups: slices of cucumber, lemon, onion or tomato; toasted French bread slices with melted cheese; dumplings; roast baby vegetables; or ravioli.

■ For smooth or cream soups: coarsely chopped herbs; contrasting coloured puréed vegetables or crème fraîche; lightly fried shredded spring onion or slices of garlic; or flavoured fried croutons.

■ For broths or consommes: finely shredded lemon zest; chiffonades of green herbs; crunchy fried noodles or shards of toasted pitta or tortilla; fine strands of shredded carrot, cucumber or red onion.

tips for top soups

■ Don't overseason: when the soup is almost ready, test for taste and then, and only then, add any necessary seasoning.

■ Buttermilk makes a lower-fat basis for a cream soup; likewise, puréed vegetables can replace some of the cream or butter. Evaporated low-fat milk can also be used instead of cream.

■ Don't overcook or freeze soups that contain rice, pasta or potatoes; add these ingredients just before serving so that their texture remains slightly firm and resilient.

■ Defrost meat-based stocks in the refrigerator and always bring them to a boil before finishing the soup.

■ Some frozen soups need to be diluted and/or re-tasted for seasoning after they have thawed.

■ Small cubes of tofu can be stirred into almost-finished vegetable soups for added protein.

■ Various vegetables and herbs have particular qualities that they impart to soup, so it is best to consider them before using. For instance, celery leaves cloud a stock; carrots both darken and sweeten a broth; and the stalks of parsley, and some onions, can add a bitter flavour to stock.

stock up on the basics

These recipes can be made up to 2 days ahead and stored, covered, in the refrigerator. Be sure to remove and discard any solidified fat from the surface of the cooled stock. If the cooled stock is to be kept longer than that, freeze it in quantities appropriate to your needs. These recipes make about 2.5 litres of stock.

Roast bones and onions in hot oven until well browned.

BEEF STOCK

2kg MEATY BEEF BONES
2 MEDIUM ONIONS (300g)
2 TRIMMED CELERY STICKS (150g), CHOPPED COARSELY
2 MEDIUM CARROTS (250g), CHOPPED COARSELY
3 BAY LEAVES
2 TEASPOONS BLACK PEPPERCORNS
5 LITRES WATER
3 LITRES WATER, EXTRA

1 Place bones and unpeeled coarsely chopped onions in baking dish. Roast, uncovered, in hot oven for about 1 hour or until bones and onions are well browned.
2 Transfer bones and onions to large saucepan; add celery, carrot, bay leaves, peppercorns and the water. Simmer, uncovered, for 3 hours, skimming surface occasionally. Add the extra water; simmer, uncovered, for 1 hour, skimming surface occasionally.
3 Strain stock mixture through muslin-lined strainer into large clean bowl.

Skim froth from the surface of the simmering stock.

Strain the stock through fine muslin to remove solids.

FISH STOCK

1.5kg FISH BONES
3 LITRES WATER
1 MEDIUM ONION (150g), CHOPPED
2 TRIMMED CELERY STICKS (150g), CHOPPED COARSELY
2 BAY LEAVES
1 TEASPOON BLACK PEPPERCORNS

1   Combine ingredients in large saucepan. Simmer, uncovered, 20 minutes; strain as in Beef Stock.

CHICKEN STOCK

2kg CHICKEN BONES
2 MEDIUM ONIONS (300g), CHOPPED COARSELY
2 TRIMMED CELERY STICKS (150g), CHOPPED COARSELY
2 MEDIUM CARROTS (250g), CHOPPED COARSELY
3 BAY LEAVES
2 TEASPOONS BLACK PEPPERCORNS
5 LITRES WATER

1   Combine ingredients in large saucepan. Simmer, uncovered, 2 hours; strain as in Beef Stock.

VEGETABLE STOCK

2 LARGE CARROTS (360g), CHOPPED COARSELY
2 LARGE PARSNIPS (360g), CHOPPED COARSELY
4 MEDIUM ONIONS (600g), CHOPPED COARSELY
12 TRIMMED CELERY STICKS (900g), CHOPPED COARSELY
4 BAY LEAVES
2 TEASPOONS BLACK PEPPERCORNS
6 LITRES WATER

1   Combine ingredients in large saucepan. Simmer, uncovered, 1½ hours; strain as in Beef Stock.

accompaniments

Accompaniments
can bring a soup to life.
A chunk of crusty bread,
a scattering of croutons,
some crispy pitta or a
savoury muffin can make
a plain bowl of soup into
a satisfying meal. The
choice is ultimately up to
you as the creative cook,
but a little thought should
go into the process as
the accompaniment
should harmonise with
and complement the
individual soup's heritage,
purpose, content and
flavour.

onion focaccia

PREPARATION TIME 20 MINUTES (PLUS STANDING TIME)
COOKING TIME 25 MINUTES (PLUS COOLING TIME)

375g PLAIN FLOUR
2 TEASPOONS (7g) DRIED YEAST
20g GRATED PARMESAN CHEESE
2 TABLESPOONS COARSELY CHOPPED FRESH SAGE
3 TEASPOONS SEA SALT FLAKES
250ml WARM WATER
60ml OLIVE OIL
1 SMALL WHITE ONION (80g), SLICED THINLY

1   Sift flour in large bowl; stir in yeast, cheese, sage and 1 teaspoon of
the salt. Gradually stir in the water and 2 tablespoons of the oil. Knead
on well floured surface about 10 minutes or until smooth and elastic.
2   Place on greased oven tray; press into a 24cm-round. Cover with
greased cling film; stand in warm place until dough doubles in size.
3   Meanwhile combine onion, remaining salt and remaining oil in small
bowl. Remove cling film from dough; sprinkle dough with onion mixture.
Bake, uncovered, in hot oven about 25 minutes or until cooked when
tested; cool on wire rack.

SERVES 8
PER SERVING 8.2g FAT; 239 CAL (999KJ)

irish soda bread

PREPARATION TIME 10 MINUTES
COOKING TIME 50 MINUTES

420g WHOLEMEAL PLAIN FLOUR
375g WHITE PLAIN FLOUR
1 TEASPOON SALT
1 TEASPOON BICARBONATE OF SODA
680ml BUTTERMILK, APPROXIMATELY

1   Sift flours, salt and soda into large bowl; return husks from sieve to bowl. Stir in enough of the buttermilk to mix to a firm dough.
2   Knead dough on floured surface until just smooth. Shape dough into 20cm round; place on greased oven tray.
3   Using sharp knife, cut 1cm-deep cross into top of dough. Bake, uncovered, in moderate oven about 50 minutes. Lift onto wire rack to cool.

MAKES 1 LOAF

rosemary bread

PREPARATION TIME 20 MINUTES
COOKING TIME 45 MINUTES

60g BUTTER
1 MEDIUM ONION (150g), CHOPPED FINELY
450g SELF-RAISING FLOUR
2 TABLESPOONS FINELY CHOPPED FRESH ROSEMARY
125g GRATED CHEDDAR CHEESE
310ml WATER, APPROXIMATELY

1   Melt 15g of the butter in small frying pan. Cook onion, stirring over medium heat about 2 minutes or until onion is soft; cool.
2   Sift flour into large bowl; rub in remaining butter. Stir in onion mixture, rosemary and two-thirds of the cheese; make well in centre. Stir in enough of the water to mix to a soft dough; knead on lightly floured surface until smooth.
3   Place dough onto greased oven tray; pat into 16cm circle. Using sharp knife, cut 1cm deep cross in top of dough. Brush with a little extra milk; sprinkle with remaining cheese.
4   Bake, uncovered, in moderate oven about 40 minutes or until bread is golden brown and sounds hollow when tapped.

MAKES 1 LOAF

corn bread

PREPARATION TIME 25 MINUTES
(PLUS STANDING TIME)
COOKING TIME 20 MINUTES

2 TEASPOONS (7g) DRIED YEAST
125ml WARM WATER
125ml WARM MILK
300g PLAIN FLOUR
85g POLENTA
½ TEASPOON SALT
2 TEASPOONS POLENTA, EXTRA

1 Mix yeast with the water in small bowl; stir in
milk. Sift flour into large bowl; stir in polenta and
salt. Stir in yeast mixture; mix to a firm dough.
Knead dough on floured surface about 10 minutes
or until dough is smooth and elastic; place dough
in greased large bowl. Cover; stand in warm place
about 1 hour or until doubled in size.
2 Turn dough onto floured surface; knead further
5 minutes. Shape dough into 13cm round; place on
lightly greased oven tray. Using sharp knife, cut 1cm
deep cross into top of dough. Stand, covered, in
warm place 20 minutes; sprinkle with extra polenta.
3 Bake, uncovered, in moderately hot oven for
about 20 minutes or until bread sounds hollow
when tapped.

MAKES 1 LOAF

beer bread

PREPARATION TIME 20 MINUTES
COOKING TIME 50 MINUTES

485g SELF-RAISING FLOUR
2 TEASPOONS SALT
2 TEASPOONS SUGAR
375ml BOTTLE LIGHT BEER

1 Grease 14cm x 21cm loaf tin; line base with
baking parchment.
2 Sift flour, salt and sugar into medium bowl;
make well in centre. Pour in beer all at once; using
spoon, mix to a soft, sticky dough.
3 Knead dough on floured surface until smooth;
divide in half. Knead each half; place in prepared tin.
4 Bake, uncovered, in moderate oven about
50 minutes or until bread is browned and sounds
hollow when tapped.
5 Turn onto wire rack; serve warm or cold.

MAKES 1 LOAF

TIP Rosemary bread, corn bread and beer
bread can be made 3 hours ahead and stored
at room temperature.

pagnotta

PREPARATION TIME 25 MINUTES
(PLUS STANDING TIME)
COOKING TIME 40 MINUTES

2 TEASPOONS DRIED YEAST
½ TEASPOON SUGAR
2 TEASPOONS SALT
525g PLAIN FLOUR
310ml SKIMMED MILK, WARMED
1 TABLESPOON OLIVE OIL

1 Combine yeast, sugar, salt and flour in large
bowl. Gradually stir in milk and half of the oil
until combined.
2 Knead dough on lightly floured surface about
2 minutes. Place dough in large oiled bowl; turn
to coat in oil. Cover; stand in warm place about
30 minutes or until dough doubles in size.
3 Turn dough onto floured surface; knead about
10 minutes until dough is smooth and elastic. Shape
dough into 58cm log; place on an oiled, floured
oven tray. Lightly brush ends with water; gently
press together to form a ring. Combine remaining oil and 2 teaspoons warm water in small bowl;
brush over dough. Sift over a little extra plain flour.
4 Place in cold oven; set temperature to moderately hot. Bake, uncovered, about 40 minutes or
until cooked when tested; cool on wire rack.

SERVES 6

herbed olive bread

PREPARATION TIME 25 MINUTES
(PLUS STANDING TIME)
COOKING TIME 45 MINUTES

4 TEASPOONS (14g) DRIED YEAST
1 TEASPOON SUGAR
310ml WARM MILK + 250ml WARM WATER
300g PLAIN FLOUR, SIFTED
80ml OLIVE OIL
525g PLAIN SIFTED FLOUR, EXTRA
1 TEASPOON SALT
150g PITTED BLACK OLIVES, HALVED
2 TABLESPOONS SHREDDED FRESH SAGE LEAVES
2 TABLESPOONS CHOPPED FRESH OREGANO

1 Combine yeast, sugar, milk and water in large
bowl, whisk until yeast is dissolved. Whisk in flour,
cover, stand in warm place about 30 minutes or
until mixture is doubled in size.
2 Stir in oil, then extra flour and salt. Turn onto
floured surface, knead about 10 minutes until
dough is smooth and elastic. Place in large greased
bowl, cover, stand in warm place about 1 hour
until dough has doubled in size. Turn onto floured
surface, knead in remaining ingredients.
3 Roll into 30cm x 35cm oval. Fold almost in half,
transfer to large greased oven tray, shape into an
oval. Cover; stand in warm place about 45 minutes
until dough has increased in size by half. Sift about
another 2 tablespoons of flour over dough, bake in
moderately hot oven about 45 minutes.

MAKES 1 LOAF

cheese & onion muffins

PREPARATION TIME 15 MINUTES (PLUS CHILLING TIME) COOKING TIME 25 MINUTES

35g PLAIN FLOUR
20g BUTTER
1 TEASPOON WATER, APPROXIMATELY
1 TABLESPOON VEGETABLE OIL
1 MEDIUM (150g) ONION, HALVED, SLICED
260g SELF-RAISING FLOUR
110g PLAIN FLOUR, EXTRA
90g GRATED CHEDDAR CHEESE
1 TABLESPOON CHOPPED FRESH CHIVES
1 EGG, LIGHTLY BEATEN
310ml BUTTERMILK
125ml VEGETABLE OIL, EXTRA

1   Place plain flour into small bowl, rub in butter; mix in just enough water to bind ingredients. Press dough into a ball, cover, freeze about 30 minutes or until firm. Grease 6 hole (180ml capacity) muffin tin. Heat oil in frying pan, add onion, cook, stirring, until soft and lightly browned; cool.
2   Sift self-raising and extra plain flour into large bowl, stir in half the onion, half the cheese and all the chives, then egg, buttermilk and extra oil.
3   Spoon mixture into prepared tin. Grate frozen dough into small bowl, quickly mix in remaining onion and cheese; sprinkle over muffins. Bake in moderately hot oven about 25 minutes.

MAKES 6

pastrami & sage scones

PREPARATION TIME 15 MINUTES
COOKING TIME 20 MINUTES

225g WHITE SELF-RAISING FLOUR
80g WHOLEMEAL SELF-RAISING FLOUR
15g BUTTER
2 TABLESPOONS CHOPPED FRESH SAGE LEAVES
60g PASTRAMI, CHOPPED
250ml MILK, APPROXIMATELY

1   Grease 20cm round sandwich cake tin. Sift flours into medium bowl, rub in butter; stir in sage and pastrami. Stir in enough milk to mix to a soft, sticky dough.
2   Turn dough onto floured surface, knead until smooth. Press dough out to 2cm thickness, cut into 5cm rounds, place into prepared tin.
3   Bake in hot oven about 20 minutes.

MAKES 12

TIP As a variation, try using some chopped ham or some cooked chopped bacon instead of the pastrami.

lamb soups

wintry lamb & vegetable soup

PREPARATION TIME 20 MINUTES
COOKING TIME 1 HOUR 45 MINUTES

4 LAMB SHANKS (1kg)
2 MEDIUM CARROTS (240g), CHOPPED COARSELY
2 MEDIUM WHITE ONIONS (300g), CHOPPED COARSELY
2 CLOVES GARLIC, CRUSHED
2 MEDIUM POTATOES (400g), CHOPPED COARSELY
2 TRIMMED CELERY STALKS (200g), CHOPPED COARSELY
400g CAN CHOPPED TOMATOES
1.5 LITRES BEEF OR CHICKEN STOCK
125ml TOMATO PASTE
2 MEDIUM COURGETTES (240g), CHOPPED COARSELY

1 Combine lamb, carrot, onion, garlic, potato, celery, undrained tomatoes, stock and paste in large saucepan. Bring to a boil, reduce heat; simmer, covered, 1 hour.
2 Add courgettes and simmer, uncovered, further 30 minutes or until lamb is tender.
3 Remove lamb from soup. When cool enough to handle, remove meat from bones, discard bones. Return meat to soup, stir until heated through.

SERVES 4
PER SERVING 9.2g FAT; 362 CAL (1513KJ)

TIP Recipe can be made three days ahead; keep, covered, in refrigerator.

lamb & black-eye bean soup

PREPARATION TIME 35 MINUTES (PLUS STANDING TIME)
COOKING TIME 3 HOURS 40 MINUTES

400g BLACK-EYE BEANS
2 MEDIUM RED PEPPERS (400g)
1 TABLESPOON OLIVE OIL
1.5kg LAMB SHANKS, TRIMMED
1 MEDIUM ONION (150g),
CHOPPED COARSELY
2 CLOVES GARLIC, QUARTERED
2 MEDIUM CARROTS (240g),
CHOPPED COARSELY
2 TRIMMED CELERY STICKS (150g),
CHOPPED COARSELY
2 TABLESPOONS TOMATO PASTE
250ml DRY RED WINE
3.5 LITRES WATER
1 TABLESPOON COARSELY
CHOPPED FRESH CORIANDER
LEAVES

1   Place black-eye beans in medium bowl, cover with water; soak overnight, drain.
2   Quarter peppers, remove and discard seeds and membranes. Roast under grill or in very hot oven, skin-side up, until skin blisters and blackens. Cover pepper pieces in plastic or paper for 5 minutes, peel away skin; chop finely.
3   Heat oil in large saucepan; cook lamb, in batches, until browned all over. Cook onion and garlic in same pan, stirring, until onion softens. Add carrot and celery; cook, stirring, 2 minutes. Add paste and wine, bring to a boil; simmer, uncovered, 5 minutes.
4   Add lamb and the water to pan; bring to a boil. Simmer, uncovered, 2 hours, skimming occasionally; strain through muslin-lined strainer into large bowl. Reserve lamb and stock; discard solids.
5   When cool enough to handle, remove lamb meat from shanks; discard bones, shred lamb.
6   Return soup to same cleaned pan with beans, lamb and pepper; stir over heat until hot. Just before serving soup, stir in coriander.

SERVES 6
PER SERVING 12.5g FAT; 1075KJ

BLACK-EYE BEANS
Often called black-eye peas, this small bone-coloured legume has a tiny black speck of an 'eye' in the curve of one side. It is good in salads and on its own, as well as in meat stews and soups like this recipe.

TIP Turn the lamb so it browns all over, ensuring that the soup is as flavoursome as possible.

meatball soup
with crispy pitta

PREPARATION TIME 15 MINUTES COOKING TIME 40 MINUTES

500g MINCED LAMB
1 TEASPOON GROUND ALLSPICE
½ TEASPOON GROUND NUTMEG
125ml OLIVE OIL
1.25 LITRES CHICKEN STOCK
50g WHITE LONG-GRAIN RICE
125ml HOT WATER
1 TABLESPOON TOMATO PASTE
3 TABLESPOONS, FINELY
CHOPPED FRESH FLAT-LEAF
PARSLEY

CRISPY PITTA
1 LARGE PITTA BREAD
¼ TEASPOON CAYENNE PEPPER

1   Combine lamb and spices in medium bowl; using hands, knead until meat mixture forms a smooth paste. Shape level teaspoons of meat mixture into balls.
2   Heat oil in large frying pan; cook meatballs, in batches, until just browned.
3   Place stock in large saucepan, bring to a boil; stir in rice and the combined hot water and tomato paste. Reduce heat, add meatballs; simmer soup, uncovered, about 30 minutes or until meatballs are cooked through. Just before serving, stir in parsley. Serve topped with crispy pitta.

CRISPY PITTA Split pitta in half; sprinkle split side with cayenne pepper. Place both rounds, split-side up, on oven trays. Bake in moderately hot oven about 10 minutes or until crisp, cool slightly before breaking into small pieces.

SERVES 4
PER SERVING 38.9g FAT; 2373KJ

lamb shank soup

PREPARATION TIME 40 MINUTES (PLUS STANDING AND
REFRIGERATION TIME) COOKING TIME 2 HOURS 50 MINUTES

300g DRIED CHICKPEAS
1 TABLESPOON OLIVE OIL
1.5kg FRENCH-TRIMMED LAMB SHANKS
1 MEDIUM ONION (150g), CHOPPED FINELY
2 MEDIUM CARROTS (240g), CHOPPED FINELY
2 TRIMMED CELERY STALKS (200g), SLICED THINLY
2 CLOVES GARLIC, CRUSHED
1 TEASPOON GROUND CUMIN
500ml CHICKEN STOCK
1 LITRE WATER
8 LARGE STALKS SWISS CHARD (400g), CHOPPED FINELY
60ml LEMON JUICE

1   Place chickpeas in medium bowl, cover with water; stand overnight.
Rinse under cold water; drain.
2   Meanwhile, heat oil in large saucepan; cook lamb, in batches, until browned.
Cook onion, carrot, celery, garlic and cumin in same pan, stirring, about
5 minutes or until onion softens. Return lamb to pan with stock and the
water; bring to a boil. Reduce heat; simmer, covered, 2 hours.
3   Remove soup mixture from heat; when lamb is cool enough to handle,
remove meat, chop coarsely. Refrigerate cooled soup mixture and lamb
meat, covered separately, overnight.
4   Discard fat from surface of soup mixture. Place soup mixture, meat and
chickpeas in large saucepan; bring to a boil. Reduce heat; simmer, covered,
30 minutes. Add swiss chard and lemon; simmer, uncovered, until swiss chard
just wilts. Serve soup with a warmed loaf of ciabatta, if desired.

SERVES 4
PER SERVING 28.2g FAT; 635 CAL (2654KJ)

SWISS CHARD is all
too often given short
shrift over another green
leafy vegetable, spinach.
Also known as silverbeet
or blettes, it's a member
of the beet family rather
than the spinach family,
a fact reflected in the
robust texture of its
leaves and wide edible
stems (which are delicious
in their own right). It suits
the flavours of the Medi-
terranean menu – garlic,
sultanas, tomato, pine nuts,
lemon and olive oil – and
it makes a great Turkish
soup with lentils, yogurt
and lemon juice.

TIPS Think about using lamb shanks that have not been french-trimmed or use 2kg lamb neck chops in this soup. The money saved will more than make up for any extra effort expended trimming excess fat from the meat before you cook it or skimming fat off the soup's surface.

■ You need 1kg of un-trimmed swiss chard to get the amount of trimmed swiss chard required for this recipe..

lamb & barley soup

PREPARATION TIME 15 MINUTES
COOKING TIME 1 HOUR 25 MINUTES

1.5kg FRENCH-TRIMMED LAMB SHANKS
3 LITRES WATER
150g PEARL BARLEY
1 MEDIUM CARROT (120g), SLICED THINLY
1 MEDIUM LEEK (350g), SLICED THINLY
2 TRIMMED CELERY STALKS (200g), SLICED THINLY
1 TABLESPOON CURRY POWDER
250g TRIMMED SWISS CHARD, CHOPPED COARSELY

1   Combine lamb, the water and barley in large saucepan; bring to a boil. Reduce heat; simmer, uncovered, 1 hour, skimming surface and stirring occasionally. Add carrot, leek and celery; simmer, uncovered, 10 minutes.

2   Remove lamb from soup mixture. When cool enough to handle, remove meat; chop coarsely. Discard bones and any fat or skin.

3   Dry-fry curry powder in small saucepan until fragrant. Return meat to soup with curry powder and swiss chard; cook, uncovered, until swiss chard wilts.

SERVES 6
PER SERVING 13.3g FAT; 336 CAL (1404KJ)

TIPS Drained canned chickpeas can be substituted for dried chickpeas.

■ Two 400g cans of tomatoes can be substituted for the fresh tomatoes.

This hearty lamb and vegetable soup originating from Morocco is traditionally eaten during the four weeks of Ramadan, after sundown, to break the day's fast.

harira

100g DRIED CHICKPEAS
500g BONED SHOULDER OF LAMB
2 TABLESPOONS OLIVE OIL
1 LARGE ONION (200g), CHOPPED COARSELY
2 TEASPOONS GROUND GINGER
1 TABLESPOON GROUND CUMIN
1 TEASPOON GROUND CINNAMON
2 TEASPOONS GROUND CORIANDER
6 SAFFRON THREADS
3 TRIMMED CELERY STICKS (225g), CHOPPED COARSELY
7 MEDIUM TOMATOES (1.3kg), DESEEDED, CHOPPED COARSELY
2.5 LITRES WATER
100g BROWN LENTILS
3 TABLESPOONS COARSELY CHOPPED FRESH CORIANDER LEAVES

PREPARATION TIME 20 MINUTES (PLUS SOAKING TIME)
COOKING TIME 2 HOURS 10 MINUTES

1 Place chickpeas in small bowl, cover with water; soak overnight, drain well.
2 Trim lamb of excess fat; cut into 2cm cubes.
3 Heat oil in large saucepan; cook onion, stirring, until soft. Add spices; cook, stirring, about 2 minutes or until fragrant. Add lamb and celery; cook, stirring, about 2 minutes or until lamb is coated in spice mixture. Add tomato; cook, stirring, about 10 minutes or until tomato slightly softens. Stir in the water and drained chickpeas; bring to a boil. Simmer, covered, about 1½ hours or until lamb is tender, stirring occasionally.
4 Stir in lentils; cook, covered, about 30 minutes or until lentils are just tender.
5 Just before serving, stir fresh coriander into soup.
6 Serve with lemon wedges and toasted pide.

SERVES 6
PER SERVING 15.6g FAT; 315 CAL (1317KJ)

black bean & lamb soup

PREPARATION TIME 25 MINUTES (PLUS SOAKING TIME)
COOKING TIME 1 HOUR 45 MINUTES

400g BLACK BEANS
500g BONED SHOULDER OF LAMB
1 TABLESPOON OLIVE OIL
1 LARGE RED ONION (300g),
CHOPPED FINELY
2 CLOVES GARLIC, CRUSHED
2 TRIMMED CELERY STICKS (150g),
SLICED THINLY
1 TABLESPOON GROUND CUMIN
½ TEASPOON GROUND CAYENNE
2½ LITRES WATER
400g CAN TOMATOES, CRUSHED
60ml DRY SHERRY
60ml BALSAMIC VINEGAR
3 TABLESPOONS COARSELY
CHOPPED FRESH CORIANDER
LEAVES
2 LIMES
4 RED THAI CHILLIES, DESEEDED,
CHOPPED FINELY
80ml WHITE WINE VINEGAR
125ml SOURED CREAM

1   Place beans in medium bowl, cover with water; soak overnight, drain well.

2   Trim lamb of excess fat; cut lamb into 1.5cm pieces.

3   Heat oil in large saucepan; cook onion and garlic, stirring, until onion is soft. Add lamb, celery, cumin and cayenne; cook, stirring, about 5 minutes or until spices are just fragrant.

4   Stir in the water and undrained crushed tomatoes. Bring to a boil; simmer, covered, 30 minutes. Add beans; simmer, covered, about 1 hour or until beans are tender. Stir in sherry and balsamic vinegar; cool 10 minutes.

5   Blend or process half of the soup, in batches, until puréed.

6   Combine puréed soup with coriander and remaining soup in pan; stir over heat until hot.

7   Meanwhile, cut limes into wedges. Combine chilli and wine vinegar in small bowl. Serve soup accompanied by lime wedges, chilli mixture and soured cream.

SERVES 6
PER SERVING 18.8g FAT; 420 CAL (1760KJ)

lamb soups

TIPS Black beans, also known as turtle beans, have a black skin, creamy texture and sweet flavour, and are a breed apart from Chinese black beans which are, in fact, fermented soy beans.

■ You can substitute stewing beef (or better yet, a ham bone and chicken stock) for the lamb.

scotch broth

PREPARATION TIME 30 MINUTES   COOKING TIME 1 HOUR 40 MINUTES

1kg LAMB NECK CHOPS
2.25 LITRES WATER
150g PEARL BARLEY
1 LARGE ONION (200g), DICED INTO 1cm PIECES
2 MEDIUM CARROTS (240g), DICED INTO 1cm PIECES
1 MEDIUM LEEK (350g), SLICED THINLY
160g FINELY SHREDDED SAVOY CABBAGE
60g FROZEN PEAS
2 TABLESPOONS COARSELY CHOPPED FRESH FLAT-LEAF PARSLEY

1   Combine chops with the water and barley in large saucepan; bring to a
boil. Reduce heat; simmer, covered, 1 hour, skimming fat from surface
occasionally. Add onion, carrot and leek; simmer, covered, about 30 minutes
or until vegetables are tender.
2   Remove chops from soup mixture; when cool enough to handle, remove
meat, chop coarsely. Discard bones.
3   Return meat to soup with cabbage and peas; cook, uncovered, about
10 minutes or until cabbage is tender. Sprinkle parsley over scotch broth just
before serving.

SERVES 4
PER SERVING 25.9g FAT; 545 CAL (2278KJ)

SAVOY CABBAGE
is a large-headed,
crimpled-leafed, loose-
centred member of the
same family as Brussels
sprouts, broccoli and
cauliflower. Less strong in
flavour than other
cabbages, it can be added
to soups, stews and
casseroles without fear of
it overpowering the dish.

beef soups

soupe au pistou

PREPARATION TIME 15 MINUTES (PLUS STANDING TIME)
COOKING TIME 1 HOUR 40 MINUTES

200g DRIED CANNELLINI BEANS
80ml OLIVE OIL
2 VEAL SHANKS (1.5kg), TRIMMED (OR USE BRAISING STEAK)
1 LARGE LEEK (500g), SLICED THINLY
2 LITRES WATER
500ml CHICKEN STOCK
2 TABLESPOONS TOASTED PINE NUTS
1 CLOVE GARLIC, QUARTERED
20g FINELY GRATED PARMESAN
6 TABLESPOONS FRESH BASIL LEAVES
2 MEDIUM CARROTS (240g), CHOPPED COARSELY
200g GREEN BEANS, TRIMMED, CHOPPED COARSELY

1 Place cannellini beans in large bowl, cover with cold water; stand, covered, overnight.

2 Heat 1 tablespoon of the oil in large saucepan; cook shanks, uncovered, until browned all over. Remove from pan. Cook leek in same pan, stirring, about 5 minutes or until just softened. Return shanks to pan with the water and stock; bring to a boil. Reduce heat; simmer, covered, 1 hour.

3 Meanwhile, blend or process remaining oil, nuts, garlic and cheese until combined. Add basil; process until pistou mixture forms a paste.

4 Remove shanks from soup. When cool enough to handle, remove meat from bones. Discard bones; chop meat coarsely. Return meat to soup with rinsed and drained cannellini beans; bring to a boil. Reduce heat; simmer, uncovered, 20 minutes. Add carrot; simmer, uncovered, 10 minutes. Add green beans and pistou; simmer, uncovered, 5 minutes.

5 Divide soup among serving bowls. Serve with slices of warm baguette, if desired, for dipping in soup.

SERVES 8
PER SERVING 13.5g FAT; 270 CAL (1129KJ)

PISTOU is a classic Provençal sauce, similar to pesto in origin. The traditional ingredients – garlic, fresh basil and olive oil – are pounded together to form a paste, with some recipes including tomatoes or a grated hard cheese, such as parmesan. We have added some toasted pine nuts to our recipe.

CANNELLINI BEANS You can use canned beans for this recipe if you prefer. Drain beans then rinse well under cold water before using them. Add towards the end of the cooking time along with the green beans and pistou.

TIP Chicken can be substituted for the beef in this recipe, if preferred.

Pronounced 'fah bah', this Vietnamese beef noodle soup has assumed cult status in the past decade or so, with restaurants specialising in it opening up throughout the western world. Many places serve the beef raw, allowing diners to drop it, piece by piece, into the hot broth to cook at the table

pho bo

PREPARATION TIME 40 MINUTES
COOKING TIME 2 HOURS 30 MINUTES

1.5kg BEEF BONES
2 MEDIUM ONIONS (300g), CHOPPED COARSELY
2 MEDIUM CARROTS (240g), CHOPPED COARSELY
4 TRIMMED CELERY STALKS (400g), CHOPPED COARSELY
2 CINNAMON STICKS
4 STAR ANISE
6 CARDAMOM PODS, BRUISED
10 BLACK PEPPERCORNS
2 TABLESPOONS FISH SAUCE
6 CLOVES
12cm PIECE FRESH GINGER (60g), SLICED THINLY
6 CLOVES GARLIC, SLICED THINLY
500g PIECE STEWING BEEF
4 LITRES WATER
2 TABLESPOONS SOY SAUCE
200g BEAN THREAD VERMICELLI
6 TBLESPOONS FRESH VIETNAMESE MINT LEAVES
4 FRESH SMALL RED THAI CHILLIES, SLICED THINLY
1 MEDIUM ONION (150g), SLICED THINLY, EXTRA
6 TBLESPOONS FRESH CORIANDER LEAVES
100g BEANSPROUTS

1 Preheat oven to hot (220°C/200°C fan-assisted).
2 Combine beef bones, onion, carrot and celery in large baking dish; roast, uncovered, about 45 minutes or until browned all over. Drain excess fat from dish.
3 Combine beef mixture, cinnamon, star anise, cardamom, peppercorns, fish sauce, cloves, ginger, garlic, stewing beef and the water in large saucepan. Bring to a boil; simmer, uncovered, 1½ hours, skimming occasionally. Strain through muslin-lined strainer into large bowl. Reserve broth and beef; discard bones and spices. When beef is cool enough to handle, shred finely; return with soy sauce and broth to cleaned pan.
4 Just before serving, place vermicelli in large heatproof bowl; cover with boiling water, stand 3 minutes, drain.
5 Divide vermicelli among serving bowls; top with broth and beef mixture, mint, chilli, extra onion and coriander leaves. Serve with beansprouts.

SERVES 6
PER SERVING 4.7g FAT; 257 CAL (1074KJ)

beef soups

TIP This soup will be at its most flavoursome if you marinate the beef overnight and make the soup as close to serving time as possible.

500g BEEF FILLET, SLICED THINLY
2 CLOVES GARLIC, CRUSHED
3 SPRING ONIONS, SLICED THINLY
2 TEASPOONS FISH SAUCE
1 TEASPOON SUGAR
1 RED THAI CHILLI, DESEEDED, CHOPPED FINELY
2 TEASPOONS GRATED FRESH GALANGAL
500g CHINESE WATER SPINACH
1.5 LITRES WATER
2 TABLESPOONS LEMON JUICE
3 TABLESPOONS TORN FRESH MINT LEAVES

beef & water spinach soup

PREPARATION TIME 20 MINUTES (PLUS MARINATING TIME)
COOKING TIME 10 MINUTES

1 Place beef, garlic, onion, sauce, sugar, chilli and galangal in large bowl; toss to combine. Cover; refrigerate 3 hours or overnight.
2 Trim spinach stems; crush stems with meat mallet or rolling pin. Chop leaves coarsely.
3 Bring the water to a boil in large saucepan, add spinach and beef mixture; simmer, uncovered, 2 minutes.
4 Remove soup from heat; stir in remaining ingredients.

SERVES 6
PER SERVING 3.6g FAT; 125 CAL (525KJ)

CHINESE WATER SPINACH is a mild, versatile vegetable with crunchy white stalks and tender, dark green leaves. It resembles a bunch of spinach (which can be substituted) but has longer, more flexible leaves.

TIPS Cook meatballs in soup close to serving time, to prevent soup from becoming cloudy.

■ Use commercially made stock if you don't want to make your own.

indonesian meatball soup

PREPARATION TIME 20 MINUTES
COOKING TIME 2 HOURS 15 MINUTES

2kg CHICKEN BONES (CARCASS, NECK, WINGS, ETC)
2 MEDIUM ONIONS (300g), CHOPPED COARSELY
2 TRIMMED CELERY STICKS (150g), CHOPPED COARSELY
2 MEDIUM CARROTS (250g), CHOPPED COARSELY
4 LITRES WATER
1 SMALL WHITE ONION (80g), CHOPPED FINELY
2 CLOVES GARLIC, CRUSHED
500g MINCED BEEF OR VEAL
2 TABLESPOONS KECAP MANIS
2 TABLESPOONS SOY SAUCE
80g BEANSPROUTS
4 SPRING ONIONS, SLICED THINLY

1   Combine bones, brown onion, celery, carrot and the water in large saucepan; bring to a boil. Simmer, uncovered, 2 hours; strain through muslin-lined strainer into large bowl. Reserve stock; discard bones and vegetables.
2   Using hands, combine white onion, garlic, mince, half of the kecap manis and half of the soy sauce in large bowl; roll rounded teaspoons of veal mixture into balls. Place on tray, cover; refrigerate 30 minutes.
3   Combine remainder of both sauces with stock in large saucepan; bring to a boil. Add meatballs; simmer, uncovered, stirring occasionally, about 10 minutes or until meatballs are cooked through.
4   Divide soup among serving bowls; top with beansprouts and spring onion.

SERVES 6
PER SERVING 2.1g FAT; 243 CAL (1016KJ)

One of the most famous of all Russian soups, borscht can be served hot or cold, puréed or chunky, meatless or replete with shredded beef, chicken or pork. This version, a traditional Ukrainian borscht, is based on a strong-flavoured beef stock, acidulated with lemon or vinegar, and always served hot

borscht

PREPARATION TIME 30 MINUTES
COOKING TIME 1 HOUR 30 MINUTES

2kg BUNCH FRESH UNCOOKED BEETROOT (ABOUT 6 BEETROOT)
50g BUTTER
2 MEDIUM ONIONS (300g), CHOPPED FINELY
2 MEDIUM POTATOES (400g), CHOPPED COARSELY
400g CAN TOMATOES
2 MEDIUM CARROTS (240g), CHOPPED COARSELY
2.5 LITRES WATER
80ml RED WINE VINEGAR
500g PIECE STEWING BEEF
3 BAY LEAVES
320g SHREDDED SAVOY CABBAGE (SEE PAGE 24)
125ml SOURED CREAM
2 TABLESPOONS FINELY CHOPPED FRESH FLAT-LEAF PARSLEY

1 Discard beetroot leaves and stems; peel and coarsely grate raw beetroot.
2 Melt butter in large saucepan; cook onion, stirring, until soft. Add beetroot, potato, undrained crushed tomatoes, carrot, the water, vinegar, beef and bay leaves. Bring to a boil; simmer, covered, 1 hour.
3 Remove and discard fat from surface of soup mixture. Remove beef from soup, shred beef then return to soup with cabbage; simmer, uncovered, 20 minutes.
4 Ladle soup into serving bowls; divide soured cream and parsley among bowls.

SERVES 6
PER SERVING 18.8g FAT; 428 CAL (1794KJ)

TIP To avoid staining your hands, wear disposable kitchen gloves when peeling beetroot then grate it using a food processor.

TIPS Do not deseed the chillies if you prefer a spicier soup.

■ Passing the soup through a food mill (sometimes called a mouli) will result in a velvety smooth texture.

■ You can use any short pasta in place of the fusilli – try farfalle or penne.

CHIFFONADE OF BASIL

1 Wash the basil then carefully remove eight of the largest leaves from stems.

2 Stack the leaves on top of one another; grip firmly and roll into tight cigar shape.

3 Using a sharp knife, cut across the 'cigar' into the thinnest possible of slices.

4 Gently unravel the finely sliced whorls of basil with your fingers: this is known as a chiffonade.

italian meatball soup

PREPARATION TIME 30 MINUTES   COOKING TIME 30 MINUTES

I TABLESPOON OLIVE OIL
2 MEDIUM ONIONS (300g), CHOPPED COARSELY
3 CLOVES GARLIC, QUARTERED
10 MEDIUM TOMATOES (APPROXIMATELY 2kg), CHOPPED COARSELY
750ml VEGETABLE STOCK
4 RED THAI CHILLIES, DESEEDED, CHOPPED FINELY
2 TABLESPOONS TOMATO PASTE
250g FUSILLI PASTA
8 FRESH BASIL LEAVES, SHREDDED FINELY

MEATBALLS
500g MINCED BEEF
2 TEASPOONS FINELY CHOPPED FRESH OREGANO

1 Heat oil in large saucepan; cook onion and garlic, stirring, until onion softens.
2 Add tomato, stock, chilli and paste; bring to a boil. Simmer, uncovered, stirring occasionally, about 15 minutes or until tomato is pulpy.
3 Blend or process tomato mixture, in batches, until puréed; push through food mill or large sieve into same cleaned pan.
4 Return soup to heat; bring to a boil. Add meatballs; simmer, uncovered, about 10 minutes or until meatballs are cooked through.
5 Meanwhile, cook pasta in large saucepan of boiling water, uncovered, until just tender; drain.
6 Just before serving soup, stir in pasta and basil.

MEATBALLS Using hands, combine beef and oregano in large bowl; roll level tablespoons of mixture into balls. Place meatballs on tray, cover; refrigerate 30 minutes.

SERVES 6
PER SERVING 7.4G FAT; 353 CAL (1476KJ)

chicken soups

chicken laksa

PREPARATION TIME 30 MINUTES (PLUS COOLING TIME) COOKING TIME 45 MINUTES

1 LITRE WATER
12 FRESH KAFFIR LIME LEAVES
2 CLOVES GARLIC, QUARTERED
800g CHICKEN THIGH FILLETS
150g LAKSA PASTE
800ml COCONUT MILK
2 FRESH RED THAI CHILLIES, CHOPPED FINELY
150g DRIED RICE STICK NOODLES
175g SINGAPORE NOODLES
2 TABLESPOONS GRATED PALM SUGAR
80ml LIME JUICE
2 TABLESPOONS FISH SAUCE
80g FRIED TOFU PUFFS, HALVED
120g BEANSPROUTS
6 TABLESPOONS FRESH CORIANDER LEAVES
6 TABLESPOONS FRESH VIETNAMESE MINT LEAVES

1 Place the water in large saucepan; bring to a boil. Add 4 lime leaves, garlic and chicken, reduce heat; simmer, covered, about 15 minutes or until chicken is cooked through. Cool chicken in liquid 15 minutes. Slice chicken thinly; reserve. Strain stock through muslin-lined sieve or colander into large bowl; discard solids. Allow stock to cool; skim fat from surface.

2 Cook paste in large saucepan, stirring, until fragrant. Stir in stock, coconut milk, chilli and remaining torn lime leaves; bring to a boil. Reduce heat; simmer, uncovered, 20 minutes.

3 Meanwhile, place rice stick noodles in large heatproof bowl, cover with boiling water, stand until just tender; drain. Place singapore noodles in separate large heat-proof bowl, cover with boiling water; separate with fork; drain. Divide both noodles among serving bowls.

4 Stir sugar, juice, sauce, tofu and chicken into laksa. Ladle laksa over noodles; sprinkle with combined sprouts and herbs.

SERVES 4
PER SERVING 59.4g FAT; 935 CAL (3908KJ)

TIPS Commercial laksa pastes vary dramatically in their heat intensity so, while we call for 150g here, you might try using less of the laksa paste you've purchased until you can determine how hot it makes the final dish.

TIPS Any pasta noodle can be substituted for the tagliatelle: a traditional Eastern European inclusion is spaetzle – tiny, wriggly noodles made by pushing a flour, egg and milk batter through a sieve directly into the soup.

■ Omit the parsnip and turnip, if desired, and add a handful of shelled fresh baby peas to the soup when you add the pasta.

Immigrants from Eastern Europe to America brought with them the belief that chicken noodle soup was 'good for what ails you', and it soon became commonly called Jewish penicillin (a name that exists to this day, as manifestly confirmed in the best-selling series of *Chicken Soup for the Soul* books). We actually used tagliatelle in our version of this recipe because its narrow width and delicate texture make it a natural for this healthy soup.

chicken noodle soup

PREPARATION TIME 15 MINUTES
COOKING TIME 2 HOURS 45 MINUTES

1.6kg WHOLE CHICKEN
4 LITRES WATER
1 MEDIUM ONION (150g), CHOPPED COARSELY
2 TRIMMED CELERY STICKS (150g), CHOPPED COARSELY
2 MEDIUM CARROTS (240g), CHOPPED COARSELY
2 CLOVES GARLIC, CRUSHED
2 BAY LEAVES
10 BLACK PEPPERCORNS
1 MEDIUM PARSNIP (125g), CHOPPED COARSELY
1 MEDIUM TURNIP (215g), CHOPPED COARSELY
125g TAGLIATELLE
2 TABLESPOONS COARSELY CHOPPED FRESH FLAT-LEAF PARSLEY
1 TABLESPOON COARSELY CHOPPED FRESH DILL

1 Combine chicken with the water, onion, celery, carrot, garlic, bay leaves and peppercorns in large saucepan. Bring to a boil; simmer, uncovered, 1½ hours, skimming fat from surface occasionally. Strain through muslin-lined strainer into large bowl; reserve broth, chicken and vegetables, discard bay leaves. When chicken is cool enough to handle, remove and discard skin and bones; chop meat finely.
2 Return chicken, vegetables and broth to same cleaned pan; bring to a boil. Add parsnip and turnip; simmer, uncovered, about 30 minutes or until parsnip and turnip are both tender.
3 Add pasta; cook, stirring, about 10 minutes or until just tender.
4 Just before serving, stir parsley and dill into soup.

SERVES 6
PER SERVING 6.4g FAT; 281 CAL (1178KJ)

chicken soups

chilli chicken & corn soup

2 TABLESPOONS OLIVE OIL
340g CHICKEN BREAST FILLETS
1 MEDIUM RED ONION (170g), CHOPPED FINELY
1 TABLESPOON PLAIN FLOUR
1.5 LITRES CHICKEN STOCK
500ml TOMATO JUICE
420g CAN CORN KERNELS, DRAINED
2 RED THAI CHILLIES, DESEEDED, CHOPPED FINELY
3 TABLESPOONS FRESH CORIANDER LEAVES

1 Heat half of the oil in large saucepan. Cook chicken until cooked through; when cool enough to handle, shred into small pieces.
2 Heat remaining oil in same pan; cook onion, stirring, until soft. Add flour; cook, stirring, until mixture bubbles and thickens. Gradually stir in stock and juice; cook, stirring, until mixture boils and thickens.
3 Add chicken, corn and chilli; stir over heat until soup is hot. Just before serving soup, stir in coriander.

SERVES 6
PER SERVING 8.5g FAT; 252 CAL (1054KJ)

chicken soups

TIPS This soup makes a lively beginning to a Mexican meal.
■ A purchased barbecued chicken can be substituted for the chicken breasts; discard skin, excess fat and all bones before shredding the meat.

TIP Remove all excess fat from chicken before cooking.

■ Serve soup with steamed jasmine rice and a side plate of fresh mint leaves, beansprouts and lime wedges.

This is the traditional creamy coconut and chicken soup we've all eaten, either in Thailand or at our favourite local Thai restaurant – now you can make it yourself and enjoy it more often.

2 TEASPOONS GROUNDNUT OIL
1 TABLESPOON FINELY CHOPPED LEMONGRASS
1 TABLESPOON GRATED FRESH GALANGAL
2 TEASPOONS GRATED FRESH GINGER
1 CLOVE GARLIC, CRUSHED
3 RED THAI CHILLIES, DESEEDED, CHOPPED FINELY
4 KAFFIR LIME LEAVES, SLICED FINELY
¼ TEASPOON GROUND TURMERIC
660ml COCONUT MILK
1 LITRE CHICKEN STOCK
500ml WATER
1 TABLESPOON FISH SAUCE
500g CHICKEN THIGH FILLETS, SLICED THINLY
3 SPRING ONIONS, CHOPPED FINELY
2 TABLESPOONS LIME JUICE
1 TABLESPOON COARSELY CHOPPED FRESH CORIANDER LEAVES

chicken & coconut soup

PREPARATION TIME 20 MINUTES   COOKING TIME 30 MINUTES

1 Heat oil in large saucepan; cook lemongrass, galangal, ginger, garlic, chilli, lime leaves and turmeric, stirring, about 2 minutes or until fragrant.
2 Stir in coconut milk, stock, the water and fish sauce; bring to a boil. Add chicken; simmer, uncovered, about 20 minutes or until chicken is cooked through and soup liquid reduced slightly.
3 Just before serving, stir onion, juice and coriander into soup.

SERVES 6
PER SERVING 30.8g FAT; 396 CAL (1657KJ)

chicken & chorizo gumbo

PREPARATION TIME 30 MINUTES
COOKING TIME 2 HOURS 15 MINUTES

1.5kg CHICKEN

1 MEDIUM ONION (150g), CHOPPED COARSELY

2 MEDIUM CARROTS (240g), CHOPPED COARSELY

2 TRIMMED CELERY STICKS (150g), CHOPPED COARSELY

1 BAY LEAF

12 BLACK PEPPERCORNS

3 LITRES WATER

60g BUTTER

2 CLOVES GARLIC, CRUSHED

1 SMALL ONION (80g), CHOPPED FINELY

1 MEDIUM RED PEPPER (200g), CHOPPED FINELY

1 TEASPOON SWEET PAPRIKA

¼ TEASPOON GROUND CAYENNE

¼ TEASPOON GROUND CLOVES

2 TEASPOONS DRIED OREGANO

35g PLAIN FLOUR

60g TOMATO PASTE

2 TABLESPOONS WORCESTERSHIRE SAUCE

400g CAN TOMATOES

200g FRESH OKRA

200g WHITE LONG-GRAIN RICE

200g CHORIZO SAUSAGE, SLICED THINLY

1   Rinse chicken under cold water, pat dry with absorbent paper.
2   Combine chicken, medium onion, carrot, celery, bay leaf, peppercorns and the water in large saucepan; bring to a boil. Simmer, covered, 1½ hours, skimming occasionally; strain through muslin-lined strainer into large bowl. Reserve stock and chicken; discard vegetables.
3   When chicken is cool enough to handle, remove and discard skin. Remove chicken meat from carcass; shred meat, discard bones.
4   Melt butter in large saucepan; cook garlic and small onion, stirring, until onion is soft. Add red pepper, paprika, cayenne, cloves and oregano; cook, stirring, about 2 minutes or until fragrant.
5   Stir in flour; cook, stirring, until mixture thickens and bubbles. Gradually stir in reserved stock, paste, sauce and undrained crushed tomatoes; stir until mixture boils and thickens. Stir in halved okra and rice; simmer, uncovered, stirring occasionally, about 15 minutes or until both okra and rice are tender.
6   Meanwhile, heat large non-stick frying pan; cook sausage, in batches, until browned, drain on absorbent paper.
7   Add reserved chicken and sausage; stir gumbo over heat until heated through.

SERVES 6
PER SERVING 22.2g FAT; 505 CAL (2116KJ)

GUMBO is the thick, robust soup that's one of the mainstays of Louisiana's Creole cooking – everyone who's ever visited New Orleans will have tasted gumbo. Traditionally made with andouille, a spicy smoked sausage of French descent, gumbo is just as delicious made with the more readily available chorizo.

TIP Fresh rather than canned okra should be used in gumbo (it's used to thicken the soup as well as impart flavour). Choose bright green, small, firm okra pods; large okra are generally tough and stringy. And take great pains not to overcook okra or it will break down to an unpleasantly pulpy state.

chicken & rice soup

1kg CHICKEN THIGH FILLETS, CHOPPED COARSELY
4 TRIMMED STICKS CELERY (300g), CHOPPED FINELY
1 LARGE ONION (200g), CHOPPED FINELY
2 CLOVES GARLIC, CRUSHED
1 CINNAMON STICK
1 TEASPOON CRACKED BLACK PEPPER
2 LITRES WATER
125ml LEMON JUICE
200g WHITE SHORT-GRAIN RICE
6 TABLESPOONS COARSELY CHOPPED FLAT-LEAF PARSLEY
2 TABLESPOONS SMALL FRESH MINT LEAVES

PREPARATION TIME 10 MINUTES
COOKING TIME 1 HOUR 15 MINUTES

1 Combine chicken, celery, onion, garlic, cinnamon, pepper and the water in large saucepan; bring to a boil. Reduce heat to a simmer; cook, covered, 1 hour, skimming surface occasionally.
2 Add juice and rice to soup; simmer, uncovered, stirring occasionally, until rice is tender; stir in parsley. Serve soup topped with mint.

SERVES 4
PER SERVING 18.5g FAT; 558 CAL (2337KJ)

TIP Removing the skin from the chickpeas is not essential, but it gives them a smoother texture.

moroccan chicken & chickpea soup

PREPARATION TIME 20 MINUTES COOKING TIME 50 MINUTES

2 TABLESPOONS OLIVE OIL

340g CHICKEN BREAST FILLETS

1 LARGE ONION (200g), CHOPPED FINELY

2 CLOVES GARLIC, CRUSHED

1 TABLESPOON GRATED FRESH GINGER

1½ TEASPOONS GROUND CUMIN

1½ TEASPOONS GROUND CORIANDER

1 TEASPOON GROUND TURMERIC

½ TEASPOON SWEET PAPRIKA

1 CINNAMON STICK

35g PLAIN FLOUR

1 LITRE CHICKEN STOCK

1 LITRE WATER

2 X 300g CANS CHICKPEAS, DRAINED, RINSED

2 X 400g CANS TOMATOES

2 TABLESPOONS FINELY CHOPPED PRESERVED LEMON

1 TABLESPOON COARSELY CHOPPED FRESH CORIANDER LEAVES

1   Heat half of the oil in large frying pan; cook chicken, uncovered, about 10 minutes or until browned both sides and cooked through. Drain chicken on absorbent paper; cool 10 minutes; using two forks, shred chicken coarsely.

2   Heat remaining oil in large saucepan; cook onion, garlic and ginger, stirring, until onion softens. Add cumin, ground coriander, turmeric, paprika and cinnamon; cook, stirring, until fragrant.

3   Add flour; cook, stirring, until mixture bubbles and thickens. Gradually stir in stock and the water; cook, stirring, until mixture comes to a boil. Simmer, uncovered, 20 minutes.

4   Add chickpeas and undrained crushed tomatoes, bring to a boil; simmer, uncovered, 10 minutes.

5   Add chicken and lemon; stir over heat until soup is hot. Just before serving soup, stir in fresh coriander.

SERVES 6

PER SERVING 11.3g FAT; 288 CAL (1205KJ)

chicken soups

TIP Use chicken necks or wings to make the stock rather than the chicken bones.

HOW TO FINELY CHOP AN ONION

1 Halve onion lengthways, leaving root end intact, then peel.

2 Press onion firmly on board, cut-side down; cut into 2 or 3 slices across.

3 Gripping onion, slice lengthways as thinly as possible.

4 Last, cut onion in crosshatch pattern into a fine dice.

chicken chowder

PREPARATION TIME 15 MINUTES
COOKING TIME 40 MINUTES

500ml CHICKEN STOCK
500ml WATER
400g 2 CHICKEN BREAST FILLETS
40g BUTTER
2 BACON RASHERS (140g), RIND REMOVED, CHOPPED COARSELY
1 MEDIUM ONION (150g), CHOPPED FINELY
1 CLOVE GARLIC, CRUSHED
1 MEDIUM LEEK (350g), SLICED THINLY
1 TRIMMED CELERY STALK (100g), CHOPPED FINELY
35g PLAIN FLOUR
2 MEDIUM POTATOES (400g), CHOPPED COARSELY
1 LITRE MILK
125ml DOUBLE CREAM
2 TABLESPOONS FINELY CHOPPED FRESH CHIVES

1 Bring stock and the water to a boil in medium saucepan; add chicken, return to a boil. Reduce heat; simmer, covered, about 10 minutes or until chicken is cooked through. Cool chicken in poaching liquid 10 minutes. Remove chicken from pan; discard poaching liquid (or keep for another use). Shred chicken coarsely.
2 Meanwhile, heat butter in large saucepan; cook bacon, onion, garlic, leek and celery, stirring, until vegetables soften.
3 Stir in flour; cook, stirring, 1 minute. Stir in potatoes, milk and cream; simmer, covered, about 15 minutes or until potato is just tender.
4 Add chicken and chives: cook, stirring, until heated through.

SERVES 4
PER SERVING 37.3g FAT; 651 CAL (2721KJ)

chicken & vegetable soup

PREPARATION TIME 25 MINUTES COOKING TIME 3 HOURS

1.8kg CHICKEN
1 MEDIUM CARROT (120g),
CHOPPED COARSELY
2 TRIMMED CELERY STICKS (150g),
CHOPPED COARSELY
1 MEDIUM ONION (150g),
CHOPPED COARSELY
1 BAY LEAF
1 TEASPOON BLACK PEPPERCORNS
3 LITRES WATER
1 TABLESPOON VEGETABLE OIL
1 LARGE SWEDE (450g), CHOPPED
COARSELY
2 LARGE PARSNIPS (360g), CHOPPED
FINELY
1 MEDIUM LEEK (350g), CHOPPED
FINELY
3 TRIMMED CELERY STICKS (225g),
CHOPPED FINELY, EXTRA
2 MEDIUM CARROTS (240g),
CHOPPED FINELY, EXTRA
2 TABLESPOONS COARSELY
CHOPPED FRESH PARSLEY

1 Remove and discard skin from chicken.
2 Combine chicken with carrot, celery, onion, bay leaf, peppercorns and the water in large saucepan, bring to a boil; simmer, uncovered, 2 hours.
3 Remove chicken from pan; strain vegetable mixture through muslin-lined sieve over large bowl. Discard vegetables; reserve stock. Remove meat from chicken, discard bones; chop chicken meat coarsely.
4 Skim away and discard solidified fat from surface of stock.
5 Heat oil in large saucepan; cook remaining vegetables, stirring, about 5 minutes or until leek is soft. Add stock, bring to a boil; simmer, covered, about 45 minutes or until vegetables are just tender. Return chicken to pan with parsley; simmer, uncovered, about 5 minutes or until heated through.

SERVES 8
PER SERVING 10.8g FAT; 288 CAL (1207KJ)

chicken soups

TIP It's easier to remove the meat from a chicken carcass when the chicken is still warm.

TIP Use chicken necks or wings to make the stock rather than the chicken bones.

This soup originated in the Sichuan province of western China, where it helps lend warmth on cold days. Specifically designed to stimulate the appetite for the meal to come, it is served as a course in itself near the beginning of a meal, immediately after the appetiser.

hot & sour soup

1.5kg CHICKEN BONES
4 LITRES WATER
2 MEDIUM ONIONS (300g), CHOPPED COARSELY
2 TRIMMED CELERY STICKS (150g), CHOPPED COARSELY
1 LARGE CARROT (180g), CHOPPED COARSELY
1 TABLESPOON SICHUAN PEPPERCORNS
3 BAY LEAVES
340g CHICKEN BREAST FILLETS
6 DRIED SHIITAKE MUSHROOMS
225g CAN BAMBOO SHOOTS, DRAINED, SLICED THINLY
50g PIECE FRESH GINGER, SLICED THINLY
2 TEASPOONS SESAME OIL
2 TABLESPOONS CIDER VINEGAR
2 TABLESPOONS SWEET CHILLI SAUCE
60ml SOY SAUCE
150g RICE STICK NOODLES
4 SPRING ONIONS, SLICED THINLY

PREPARATION TIME 25 MINUTES (PLUS SOAKING TIME)
COOKING TIME 2 HOURS 30 MINUTES

1 Combine chicken bones with the water, brown onion, celery, carrot, peppercorns and bay leaves in large saucepan. Bring to a boil; simmer, uncovered, 1½ hours, skimming occasionally.
2 Add chicken breast; simmer, uncovered, about 20 minutes or until chicken is cooked through. Strain through muslin-lined strainer into large bowl. Reserve stock and chicken; discard bones and vegetables. When chicken is cool enough to handle, shred finely.
3 Meanwhile, place mushrooms in small heatproof bowl, cover with boiling water, stand 10 minutes; drain. Remove and discard stems from mushrooms; slice caps thinly.
4 Return stock to same cleaned pan with mushrooms, bamboo shoots, ginger, oil, vinegar and sauces; bring to a boil. Simmer, uncovered, 15 minutes, stirring occasionally. Add shredded chicken and noodles; cook, stirring, about 5 minutes or until noodles are just tender.
5 Just before serving, add green onion to soup.

SERVES 6
PER SERVING 4.5g FAT; 164 CAL (686KJ)

clam chowder

PREPARATION TIME 15 MINUTES (PLUS STANDING TIME)
COOKING TIME 25 MINUTES

1kg BABY CLAMS
2 TABLESPOONS COARSE COOKING SALT
40g BUTTER
1 LARGE ONION (200g), CHOPPED COARSELY
2 RINDLESS BACON RASHERS (130g), CHOPPED COARSELY
1 CLOVE GARLIC, CRUSHED
2 TABLESPOONS PLAIN FLOUR
750ml MILK, WARMED
500ml VEGETABLE STOCK, WARMED
2 MEDIUM POTATOES (400g), CHOPPED COARSELY
2 TABLESPOONS FINELY CHOPPED FRESH CHIVES

1 Rinse clams under cold water; place in large bowl, sprinkle with salt, cover with water. Stand 1 hour; rinse, drain.
2 Meanwhile, melt butter in large saucepan; cook onion, bacon and garlic, stirring, until onion softens. Add flour to pan; cook, stirring, until mixture thickens and bubbles. Gradually stir in milk and stock; stir until mixture boils and thickens slightly. Add potato, reduce heat; simmer, covered, until potato is tender.
3 Add clams; simmer, covered, about 5 minutes or until clams open (discard any that do not). Remove from heat; stir in chives. Serve chowder with grilled slices of french bread, if desired.

SERVES 4
PER SERVING 19.4g FAT; 400 CAL (1672KJ)

CLAMS we used a small ridge-shelled variety of this bivalve mollusc; also known as vongole. When cooking bivalves, it is important to always rinse them well under cold running water and to discard any that do not open when cooked.

TIPS Recipe must be made and served immediately, as seafood does not reheat successfully.

■ You will need to use an extra large saucepan to fit in all the seafood.

6 SMALL, UNCOOKED CRABS (2kg)
2 TABLESPOONS OLIVE OIL
4 CLOVES GARLIC, CRUSHED
2 MEDIUM WHITE ONIONS (300g), CHOPPED FINELY
70g TOMATO PASTE
180ml DRY WHITE WINE
2 X 400g CANS CHOPPED TOMATOES
½ TEASPOON GROUND TURMERIC
2 BAY LEAVES
2 TEASPOONS WHITE SUGAR
375ml WATER
1kg FIRM WHITE FISH FILLETS, CHOPPED COARSELY
500g UNCOOKED LARGE PRAWNS
250g SCALLOPS
250g CALAMARI RINGS

bouillabaisse

PREPARATION TIME 45 MINUTES COOKING TIME 40 MINUTES

1 Remove and discard triangular flap from underside of each crab. Remove and discard the whitish gills, liver and brain matter; rinse crab well. Crack nippers slightly; chop down centre of each crab to separate body into 2 pieces.
2 Heat oil in large saucepan, add garlic and onion; cook, stirring, until onion is soft.
3 Stir in tomato paste, wine, undrained tomatoes, turmeric, bay leaves, sugar and the water. Bring to a boil, reduce heat, simmer, uncovered, 10 minutes.
4 Add crab and fish to tomato mixture, bring to a boil; reduce heat, simmer, covered, 5 minutes.
5 Meanwhile, shell and devein prawns leaving tails intact. Remove vein from scallops.
6 Stir prawns, scallops and calamari into tomato mixture, bring to a boil, reduce heat, simmer until prawns just change colour.
7 Serve bouillabaisse immediately, with fresh crusty bread, if desired.

SERVES 6
PER SERVING 11.7g FAT; 441 CAL (1843KJ)
(EXCLUDING AIOLI AND ROUILLE)

■ Born on the Mediterranean coast around Marseilles, this classic French dish was originally made by local fisherman with what was unsold of their daily catch. A main-dish seafood soup, bouillabaisse is always made using local fish, thus explaining the immense changes in overall colour and flavour among the many regional variations. Aioli, an intense garlic mayonnaise, and rouille, a red sauce made with peppers and chillies, traditionally accompany bouillabaisse wherever it is served.

AIOLI

Blend or process 4 quartered cloves garlic, 2 egg yolks and 2 tablespoons lemon juice until creamy. With motor operating, gradually add 250ml olive oil; process until aioli thickens.

ROUILLE

Quarter 2 medium red peppers, remove and discard seeds and membranes. Roast under grill or in very hot oven, skin-side up, until skin blisters and blackens. Cover in plastic or paper for 5 minutes; peel away skin, chop coarsely. Process 2 deseeded, coarsely chopped red Thai chillies, 1 quartered clove garlic and 2 tablespoons stale breadcrumbs until combined. With motor operating, gradually add 60ml olive oil; process until rouille thickens.

TIP Commercially made fish stock can be substituted for the homemade stock, but the prawn shells should still be cooked and strained, as in step 2, for the correct colour and flavour.

seafood bisque

PREPARATION TIME 30 MINUTES COOKING TIME 55 MINUTES

300g MEDIUM UNCOOKED PRAWNS
2.5 LITRES FISH STOCK
2 BAY LEAVES
3 SPRIGS FRESH FLAT-LEAF PARSLEY
60g BUTTER
3 SMALL LEEKS (600g), CHOPPED FINELY
50g PLAIN FLOUR
125ml BRANDY
80ml LEMON JUICE
300g CRAB MEAT
250ml DOUBLE CREAM
¼ TEASPOON GROUND CAYENNE
1 TABLESPOON COARSELY CHOPPED FRESH DILL

1 Shell and devein prawns, leaving tails intact. Reserve shells; chop prawn meat coarsely.
2 Combine stock, reserved shells, bay leaves and parsley in large saucepan. Bring to a boil; simmer, uncovered, 20 minutes. Strain through muslin-lined strainer into large bowl; discard solids, reserve broth.
3 Melt butter in same cleaned pan; cook leek, stirring, about 10 minutes or until soft. Stir in flour; cook, stirring, until mixture bubbles and thickens. Gradually stir in combined brandy and juice; cook, stirring, until mixture boils and thickens. Using back of spoon, push leek mixture through large sieve into large clean saucepan; discard solids in sieve.
4 Return leek mixture to heat, gradually stirring in the broth; cook, stirring, until mixture boils and thickens. Stir in crab and prawn meat; cook, stirring, 5 minutes. Just before serving, stir cream, cayenne and dill into bisque.

SERVES 6
PER SERVING 24.5G FAT; 374 CAL (1567KJ)

Seafood bisque began life as a waterfront soup – where better is there to source the copious amount of prawn shells required to give this beautiful soup its intense flavour? Nowadays, home cooks replicate the flavours of the sea by making their own bisque base using the shells from the prawns, enriching the liquid with the addition of cream.

56

TIPS You can substitute soured cream for the crème fraîche, if preferred.

■ Pick over the trout and discard even the most minuscule bone fragments.

60ml OLIVE OIL

1kg SMALL FRESH JERUSALEM ARTICHOKES (APPROXIMATELY 32), TRIMMED, PEELED

20g BUTTER

3 SHALLOTS, CHOPPED COARSELY

1 CLOVE GARLIC, QUARTERED

2 LITRES CHICKEN STOCK

2 TABLESPOONS LEMON JUICE

125ml CRÈME FRAÎCHE

1 MEDIUM SMOKED TROUT (375g), FLAKED

1 TABLESPOON FINELY GRATED LEMON RIND

smoked trout & jerusalem artichoke soup

PREPARATION TIME 30 MINUTES
COOKING TIME 1 HOUR 15 MINUTES

1 Preheat oven to hot.

2 Combine oil and artichokes in large baking dish; toss artichokes to coat with oil. Roast in hot oven, uncovered, turning occasionally, about 1 hour or until artichokes are tender.

3 Melt butter in large saucepan; cook shallot and garlic, stirring, until both just soften. Add artichokes, stock and juice; bring to a boil. Simmer, uncovered, 10 minutes; cool 10 minutes.

4 Blend or process soup mixture, in batches, until smooth.

5 Return soup to same cleaned pan; stir over heat until hot. Stir in crème fraîche and trout then divide soup among serving bowls; sprinkle each with rind.

SERVES 6
PER SERVING 24g FAT; 364 CAL (1522KJ)

JERUSALEM ARTICHOKE Looking like a knobbly parsnip, this crisp tuber has the texture of a fresh water chestnut and a unique earthy taste. It's very versatile, suiting casseroles, roasts and pies, plus it makes a wonderful cream soup. After peeling, keep submerged in acidulated water to prevent it discolouring.

seafood soups

TIP Scrub mussels with a stiff brush under cold running water.

mussels in fragrant thai broth

PREPARATION TIME 20 MINUTES   COOKING TIME 15 MINUTES

100g JASMINE RICE

1kg SMALL BLACK MUSSELS

1 TABLESPOON VEGETABLE OIL

2 TABLESPOONS THAI GREEN CURRY PASTE

375ml WATER

375ml FISH STOCK

2 TEASPOONS FISH SAUCE

2 TEASPOONS BROWN SUGAR

400ml COCONUT MILK

3 TABLESPOONS COARSELY CHOPPED FRESH CORIANDER

4 SPRING ONIONS, CHOPPED FINELY

1 TABLESPOON LIME JUICE

1   Cook rice in large saucepan of boiling water, uncovered, until just tender; drain. Cover to keep warm.
2   Meanwhile, scrub mussels; remove beards.
3   Heat oil in large saucepan; cook paste, stirring, until fragrant. Add the water, stock, sauce and sugar; bring to a boil. Add coconut milk; return to a boil. Reduce heat; simmer, stirring, 1 minute. Add mussels; cook, covered, about 5 minutes or until mussels open (discard any that do not). Remove from heat; stir in coriander, onion and juice.
4   Divide cooked rice among serving bowls; top with mussels and broth.

SERVES 4
PER SERVING 30G FAT; 425 CAL (1777KJ)

prawn laksa

PREPARATION TIME 45 MINUTES
COOKING TIME 1 HOUR 20 MINUTES

2kg MEDIUM UNCOOKED PRAWNS
1 BUNCH FRESH CORIANDER
(APPROXIMATELY 100g)
4 TRIMMED CELERY STICKS (300g),
CHOPPED COARSELY
2 MEDIUM CARROTS (240g),
CHOPPED COARSELY
2 LARGE ONIONS (400g), CHOPPED
COARSELY
3 LITRES WATER
2 STICKS LEMONGRASS, CHOPPED
COARSELY
3 RED THAI CHILLIES, DESEEDED,
CHOPPED COARSELY
1 TEASPOON GROUND TURMERIC
3 TABLESPOONS COARSELY
CHOPPED FRESH VIETNAMESE
MINT LEAVES
2 CLOVES GARLIC, CRUSHED
1 TABLESPOON GRATED FRESH
GINGER
1 TABLESPOON GRATED FRESH
GALANGAL
1 TABLESPOON SHRIMP PASTE
1 TABLESPOON GROUND
CORIANDER
2 TABLESPOONS GROUNDNUT OIL
400ml COCONUT MILK
100g FRESH SINGAPORE EGG
NOODLES
200g FRIED TOFU
100g BEANSPROUTS
4 SPRING ONIONS, SLICED THINLY

1   Shell and devein prawns; reserve shells. Cut roots from coriander; wash leaves and roots well, reserve both but keep separate.
2   Combine reserved shells, coriander roots, celery, carrot and half of the onion with the water in large saucepan. Bring to a boil; simmer, uncovered, 30 minutes. Strain through muslin-lined strainer into large bowl; reserve broth, discard shells and vegetables.
3   Blend or process remaining chopped onion with 3 tablespoons of the coriander leaves, lemongrass, chilli, turmeric, mint, garlic, ginger, galangal, shrimp paste, ground coriander and half of the oil until mixture forms a paste.
4   Heat remaining oil in large saucepan; cook laksa paste, stirring, about 2 minutes or until fragrant. Stir in reserved broth and coconut milk, bring to a boil; simmer, uncovered, 20 minutes. Stir in prawns; cook, stirring, about 10 minutes or until prawns are changed in colour.
5   Meanwhile, place noodles in large heatproof bowl, cover with boiling water; stand 3 minutes, drain. Cut tofu into 2cm cubes.
6   Just before serving, stir noodles, tofu, 2 tablespoons finely chopped coriander leaves, sprouts and spring onion into laksa.

SERVES 6
PER SERVING 25.6g FAT; 460 CAL (1926KJ)

There are several versions of this Malaysian spicy noodle soup, each of them delicious. Our recipe has its origins in the laksas of Penang, a colonial city on the north-west coast, known for the splendid variety of its seafood. Vietnamese mint leaves are called daun laksa (laksa leaves) in Malaysia, and are an integral ingredient to every laksa.

seafood soups

TIP If you don't have access to packages of fried tofu, use fresh – cut tofu into cubes then shallow-fry it in vegetable oil until browned lightly; drain on absorbent paper.

TIP You can substitute
½ teaspoon ground turmeric
for the saffron to achieve the
right colour.

oyster & saffron soup

PREPARATION TIME 20 MINUTES   COOKING TIME 45 MINUTES

80g BUTTER
1 LARGE ONION (200g), CHOPPED COARSELY
1 MEDIUM LEEK (350g), CHOPPED COARSELY
4 MEDIUM POTATOES (800g), CHOPPED COARSELY
6 SAFFRON THREADS
1.5 LITRES FISH STOCK
1 LITRE WATER
24 OYSTERS, SHELLED
125ml DOUBLE CREAM
2 TABLESPOONS LEMON JUICE
3 TABLESPOONS FINELY CHOPPED FRESH CHIVES

1   Melt butter in large saucepan; cook onion and leek, stirring,
about 10 minutes or until both soften. Add potato and saffron;
cook, stirring, 2 minutes.
2   Add stock and the water; bring to a boil. Simmer, uncovered,
about 15 minutes or until potato softens. Remove from heat, add
half of the oysters; cool 10 minutes.
3   Blend or process soup mixture, in batches, until smooth.
4   Return soup to same cleaned pan with remaining oysters,
cream and juice; stir over heat until hot. Just before serving soup,
stir in chives.

SERVES 6
PER SERVING 21.2g FAT; 320 CAL (1341KJ)

SHUCKING OYSTERS

1   Wrap a tea towel
around each oyster as
you lever a knife into the
hinge, twisting it until the
shells pop apart.
2   Loosen oyster from
shell with the tip of a
small sharp knife; try to
reserve the oyster liquor
for added natural flavour.

vegetable soups

vegetable soup

PREPARATION TIME 15 MINUTES
COOKING TIME 35 MINUTES

1 TABLESPOON VEGETABLE OIL
2 LARGE ONIONS (400g), CHOPPED FINELY
2 LARGE CARROTS (360g), CHOPPED COARSELY
8 TRIMMED CELERY STALKS (800g), CHOPPED COARSELY
3 CLOVES GARLIC, CRUSHED
1 LITRE VEGETABLE STOCK
1 LITRE WATER
165g SOUP PASTA
2 MEDIUM COURGETTES (240g), SLICED THICKLY
250g TRIMMED SWISS CHARD, CHOPPED COARSELY

1   Heat oil in large saucepan; cook onion, carrot, celery and garlic, stirring, until vegetables soften.
2   Add stock and the water; bring to a boil. Reduce heat; simmer, uncovered, 10 minutes. Add pasta and courgettes; simmer, uncovered, stirring occasionally, about 5 minutes or until pasta is tender. Add swiss chard; cook, stirring, until swiss chard just wilts.

SERVES 4
PER SERVING 6.8g FAT; 310 CAL (1296KJ)

SOUP PASTA There are many types of pasta suitable for use in soup. We used risoni, which is the regional name for a rice-shaped pastina (tiny pasta), but orzo, stelline, ditali or fedelini work just as well. If you don't have any soup pasta to hand, you can use angel-hair pasta or vermicelli broken into small pieces.

TIP You will need approximately 1kg swiss chard for this recipe.

leek & potato soup

PREPARATION TIME 10 MINUTES
COOKING TIME 25 MINUTES

4 TEASPOONS OLIVE OIL
4 CLOVES GARLIC, CRUSHED
2 TEASPOONS FRESH THYME LEAVES
4 SMALL LEEKS (800g), SLICED THINLY
4 MEDIUM POTATOES (800g),
CHOPPED COARSELY
2 LITRES VEGETABLE STOCK
2 SPRING ONIONS, SLICED THINLY

1 Heat oil in small saucepan; cook garlic, thyme and leek, stirring, about 3 minutes or until leek softens. Add potato and stock; bring to a boil. Reduce heat; simmer, covered, about 15 minutes or until potato is tender.
2 Blend or process leek mixture until smooth.
3 Reheat soup; serve soup topped with onion.

SERVES 4
PER SERVING 5.5g FAT; 243 CAL (1016KJ)

TIPS Both the leek and potato must be cooked until very soft for the requisite smoothness of this soup.

We recommend you use homemade stock for this delicate soup; the commercially packaged stocks impart conflicting flavours.

Vichyssoise is a well-known French potato and leek soup; rich and creamy, it is generally served cold.

vichyssoise

60g BUTTER

I LARGE ONION (200g), CHOPPED FINELY

2 MEDIUM LEEKS (700g), SLICED THINLY

3 LARGE POTATOES (900g), CHOPPED COARSELY

4 TRIMMED CELERY STICKS (300g), CHOPPED COARSELY

2 LITRES VEGETABLE STOCK

180ml DOUBLE CREAM

2 TABLESPOONS FINELY CHOPPED FRESH CHERVIL

PREPARATION TIME 15 MINUTES (PLUS REFRIGERATION TIME)
COOKING TIME 40 MINUTES

1 Melt butter in large saucepan; cook onion, stirring, until onion is soft. Add leek; cook, stirring, about 10 minutes or until leek is soft.
2 Add potato and celery; cook, stirring, 2 minutes. Stir in stock, bring to a boil; simmer, uncovered, about 15 minutes or until potato is soft, stirring occasionally.
3 Blend or process soup, in batches, adding cream gradually, until smoothly puréed.
4 Just before serving, sprinkle chervil over cold soup.

SERVES 6
PER SERVING 22g FAT; 376 CAL (1573KJ)

vegetable soups

cream of roasted garlic & potato soup

PREPARATION TIME 10 MINUTES
COOKING TIME 30 MINUTES

2 MEDIUM GARLIC BULBS (140g),
UNPEELED
2 TABLESPOONS OLIVE OIL
2 MEDIUM ONIONS (300g),
CHOPPED COARSELY
1 TABLESPOON FRESH THYME
LEAVES
5 MEDIUM POTATOES (1kg),
CHOPPED COARSELY
1.25 LITRES CHICKEN OR
VEGETABLE STOCK
180ml DOUBLE CREAM

1 Preheat oven to moderate (180°C/160°C fan-assisted).
2 Separate garlic bulbs into cloves; place unpeeled cloves, in single layer, on oven tray. Drizzle with half of the oil. Roast, uncovered, about 15 minutes or until garlic is soft. Remove from oven; when cool enough to handle, squeeze garlic into small bowl, discard skins.
3 Meanwhile, heat remaining oil in large saucepan; cook onion and thyme, stirring, until onion softens. Add potato; cook, stirring, 5 minutes. Add stock; bring to a boil. Reduce heat; simmer, uncovered, about 15 minutes or until potato is just tender. Stir in garlic; simmer, uncovered, 5 minutes.
4 Blend or process soup, in batches, until smooth; return to same cleaned pan. Reheat until hot; stir in cream. Divide soup among serving bowls; sprinkle with extra thyme, if desired.

SERVES 4
PER SERVING 31.3g FAT; 486 CAL (2032KJ)

TIP The amount of time the garlic is cooked makes a big difference to its pungency: the longer it's cooked, the more creamy in texture and subtly nutty in flavour it becomes.

50g BUTTER
I MEDIUM ONION (150g), CHOPPED
COARSELY
2 CLOVES GARLIC, QUARTERED
3 LARGE LEEKS (1.5kg), SLICED THINLY
2 LARGE POTATOES (600g),
CHOPPED COARSELY
750ml VEGETABLE STOCK
1.5 LITRES WATER
125ml DOUBLE CREAM
I TABLESPOON FINELY CHOPPED
FRESH GARLIC CHIVES

PARMESAN POTATO
DUMPLINGS
2 MEDIUM POTATOES (400g),
CHOPPED COARSELY
20g BUTTER
2 TABLESPOONS SOURED CREAM
20g FINELY GRATED PARMESAN
CHEESE
2 TABLESPOONS FINELY CHOPPED
FRESH GARLIC CHIVES
150g SELF-RAISING FLOUR
I EGG, BEATEN LIGHTLY

leek soup with parmesan potato dumplings

PREPARATION TIME 30 MINUTES   COOKING TIME 55 MINUTES

1 Melt butter in large saucepan; cook onion, garlic and leek, stirring, until leek softens.
2 Add potato, stock and the water; bring to a boil; simmer, covered, 25 minutes.
3 Blend or process soup mixture, in batches, until smooth.
4 Return soup to same cleaned pan; stir over heat until hot.
Drop rounded tablespoons of dumpling mixture into soup; simmer, uncovered, about 10 minutes or until dumplings are cooked through, stirring occasionally to turn dumplings. Stir in cream and chives.

PARMESAN POTATO DUMPLINGS Boil, steam or microwave potato until tender; drain. Mash potato, butter and sour cream in medium bowl until smooth; add remaining ingredients, mix well.

SERVES 6
PER SERVING 24.3g FAT; 472 CAL (1976KJ)

fresh tomato & fennel soup

PREPARATION TIME 20 MINUTES   COOKING TIME 40 MINUTES

2 MEDIUM FENNEL BULBS (1kg)
40g BUTTER
2 MEDIUM ONIONS (300g),
CHOPPED COARSELY
2 CLOVES GARLIC, QUARTERED
2kg PLUM TOMATOES, QUARTERED
20g BUTTER, EXTRA
2 CLOVES GARLIC, CRUSHED, EXTRA
750ml VEGETABLE STOCK

1   Trim fennel, discarding woody stalks and all but a handful of the fine uppermost leaves; reserve leaves. Chop about a third of the fennel finely; reserve. Chop remaining fennel coarsely.

2   Melt butter in large saucepan; cook coarsely chopped fennel, onion and garlic, stirring, until onion is soft. Add tomato; cook, uncovered, stirring occasionally, about 30 minutes or until tomato is very soft and pulpy.

3   Blend or process soup mixture, in batches, until smooth then pass through a food mill or fine sieve back into same pan.

4   Heat extra butter in small frying pan; cook extra garlic and finely chopped fennel, stirring, until fennel is just soft and golden brown. Add to soup with stock; bring to a boil.

5   Simmer about 5 minutes or until soup is hot. Just before serving, stir in finely chopped reserved fennel leaves.

SERVES 6
PER SERVING 8.9g FAT; 191 CAL (799KJ)

TIPS This refreshing soup is light enough to serve as a first course when entertaining. Since it freezes so well, make a double batch when fennel is in season – eat half now and freeze the remaining half.

If you don't own a food mill (sometimes called a mouli) or prefer to use a handheld blender, the tomatoes must be peeled.

vegetable soups

TIP The soup can be made two days ahead. The bacon toasts are best made close to serving.

cauliflower soup with cheese & bacon toasts

PREPARATION TIME 20 MINUTES   COOKING TIME 20 MINUTES

1 TABLESPOON OLIVE OIL
1 MEDIUM ONION (150g),
CHOPPED COARSELY
2 CLOVES GARLIC, CRUSHED
1 LARGE POTATO (300g),
CHOPPED FINELY
1kg CAULIFLOWER, TRIMMED,
CHOPPED COARSELY
750ml CHICKEN OR VEGETABLE
STOCK
750ml WATER
2 TABLESPOONS COARSELY
CHOPPED FRESH CHIVES

CHEESE & BACON TOASTS
3 THIN BACON RASHERS (210g),
QUARTERED
1 THIN CRUSTY ITALIAN-STYLE
BREAD
1 TABLESPOON WHOLEGRAIN
MUSTARD
120g THINLY SLICED CHEDDAR
CHEESE

1 Heat oil in large saucepan; cook onion and garlic over low heat, stirring, until soft, but not coloured.
2 Add potato, cauliflower, stock and the water, bring to a boil. Reduce heat; simmer, covered, about 15 minutes or until vegetables are very soft.
3 Meanwhile, make cheese and bacon toasts.
4 Blend or process cauliflower mixture, in batches, until smooth; return to pan, stir gently over low heat until hot.
5 Divide soup among serving bowls; sprinkle with chives. Serve with cheese and bacon toasts.

CHEESE & BACON TOASTS Place bacon on foil-covered oven tray; grill until browned and crisp. Slice bread diagonally into 12 thin slices. Grill bread slices until browned lightly; spread with mustard, top with cheese. Grill until cheese melts; top with bacon.

SERVES 6
PER SERVING 14.3g FAT; 336 CAL (1404KJ)

TIP Soup can be made 2 days ahead and kept refrigerated, covered, or frozen for up to 6 months.

roasted pumpkin & sweet potato soup

PREPARATION TIME 25 MINUTES COOKING TIME 55 MINUTES

2 LARGE ONIONS (400g)
750g PUMPKIN, CUT INTO 5cm CUBES
1 LARGE SWEET POTATO (500g),
CUT INTO 5cm CUBES
2 LARGE CARROTS (360g), CUT INTO
2cm SLICES
4 CLOVES GARLIC, PEELED
2 TEASPOONS CUMIN SEEDS
1 TEASPOON CORIANDER SEEDS
OLIVE OIL SPRAY
750ml VEGETABLE STOCK
4 TABLESPOONS FRESH CORIANDER
LEAVES

1 Peel onions and cut into eight wedges.
2 Combine vegetables in large baking dish with garlic and seeds; coat with olive oil spray.
3 Bake, uncovered, turning occasionally, about 40 minutes or until vegetables are tender and golden brown.
4 Purée vegetables with stock, in batches, in food processor or blender until smooth; strain into large saucepan. Cover; bring to a boil. Serve topped with coriander leaves.

SERVES 4
PER SERVING 3g FAT; 260 CAL (1087KJ)

sweet potato
& coriander soup

1 TEASPOON GROUNDNUT OIL
2 MEDIUM LEEKS (700g), CHOPPED
COARSELY
3 CLOVES GARLIC, QUARTERED
2 MEDIUM SWEET POTATOES (800g),
CHOPPED COARSELY
1 LITRE CHICKEN OR VEGETABLE
STOCK
160ml LIGHT EVAPORATED MILK
4 TABLESPOONS FINELY CHOPPED
FRESH CORIANDER

1   Heat oil in large saucepan; cook leek and garlic, stirring, until leek softens. Add sweet potatoes and stock; bring to a boil. Reduce heat; simmer, covered, 15 minutes or until sweet potato softens.
2   Blend or process soup, in batches, until smooth. Return soup to same cleaned pan; simmer, uncovered, until soup thickens slightly. Add evaporated milk and coriander; stir, without boiling, until heated through.
3   Divide soup among serving bowls; top with fresh coriander leaves, if desired.

SERVES 4
PER SERVING 2.9g FAT; 213 CAL (890KJ)

TIP The smoothest consis-
tency for this soup will be
achieved by using a blender,
hand-held stick blender or
a mouli.

green pea soup

PREPARATION TIME 10 MINUTES (PLUS SOAKING TIME)
COOKING TIME 1 HOUR 15 MINUTES

400g GREEN SPLIT PEAS
1 LITRE WATER
1 TABLESPOON OLIVE OIL
1 LARGE ONION (200g), CHOPPED
COARSELY
1 CLOVE GARLIC, CRUSHED
2 TRIMMED STICKS CELERY (150g),
CHOPPED COARSELY
1.25 LITRES CHICKEN OR VEGETABLE
STOCK
500g FROZEN PEAS

1   Soak split peas in the water in a large bowl for 3 hours or overnight.

2   Heat oil in large saucepan; cook onion and garlic, stirring, until onion is soft. Stir in celery; cook, stirring, 2 minutes.

3   Add undrained peas and stock, bring to a boil; simmer, uncovered, about 1 hour or until peas are tender (skimming the surface and stirring occasionally). Stir in frozen peas; cook, stirring, about 10 minutes or until peas are tender.

4   Blend or process soup, in batches, until puréed; push through food mill or large sieve into large clean saucepan.

5   Just before serving, stir over heat until soup is hot.

SERVES 6
PER SERVING 5.2g FAT; 323 CAL (1354KJ)

vegetable soups

TIP Add 300ml of double cream when processing the soup for a richer, smoother variation.

TIPS Try to get hold of some whole dried peas for this recipe, before they have been halved to make split peas.

█ If you haven't soaked the peas overnight, simply double the cooking time in step 2 to 2 hours.

pea & ham soup

PREPARATION TIME 15 MINUTES (PLUS SOAKING TIME)
COOKING TIME 1 HOUR 10 MINUTES

375g WHOLE DRIED PEAS
1 MEDIUM ONION (150g), CHOPPED COARSELY
2 TRIMMED CELERY STICKS (150g), CHOPPED COARSELY
2 BAY LEAVES
1.5kg HAM BONE
2.5 LITRES WATER
1 TEASPOON CRACKED BLACK PEPPER

1 Place peas in large bowl, cover with water; soak overnight, drain.
2 Combine peas in large saucepan with remaining ingredients; bring to a boil. Reduce heat; simmer, covered, about 1 hour or until peas are tender.
3 Remove ham bone; when cool enough to handle, remove ham from bone. Discard bone and fat; shred ham finely.
4 Blend or process half of the pea mixture, in batches, until puréed; return to pan with remaining unprocessed pea mixture and ham. Reheat soup, stirring over heat until hot.

SERVES 6
PER SERVING 4.2g FAT; 281 CAL (1178KJ)

vegetable soups

TIPS While gruyère is the traditional cheese of choice, you can substitute it with Emmenthaler or Jarlsberg.
■ The secret to getting the flavour of this soup right is in the long, slow caramelising of the onion.

french onion soup

■ This classic soup became famous almost a hundred years ago as the early morning staple of Parisienne workers in Les Halles markets. Its restorative qualities became appreciated among late-night revellers winding down at the markets, then spread to the vast hordes of tourists that descended on the French capital after the war. One of the easiest soups imaginable to make, you'll soon discover why it became – and has remained – so popular.

PREPARATION TIME 25 MINUTES COOKING TIME 35 MINUTES

50g BUTTER
6 MEDIUM ONIONS (900g), SLICED THICKLY
4 CLOVES GARLIC, CRUSHED
125ml DRY RED WINE
2 LITRES BEEF STOCK
4 SPRIGS FRESH THYME
2 BAY LEAVES
1 SMALL FRENCH BREAD STICK
125g COARSELY GRATED GRUYÈRE CHEESE

1 Melt butter in large saucepan; cook onion and garlic, stirring, about 15 minutes or until onion caramelises.
2 Stir in wine, stock, thyme and bay leaves. Bring to a boil; simmer, uncovered, 20 minutes, stirring occasionally.
3 Meanwhile, cut bread into 2cm slices, place bread on oven tray; toast under hot grill until browned lightly both sides. Divide cheese among toasted bread; grill until cheese melts and is browned lightly.
4 Just before serving, divide cheese toasts among serving bowls; pour hot onion soup over the toasts.

SERVES 6
PER SERVING 14.6g FAT; 289 CAL (1212KJ)

TIPS The stock mixture must to be taken off the heat before adding the egg mixture or the soup will curdle. There is a belief among Greek cooks that whistling when adding the egg mixture will prevent curdling.

■ Some finely shredded poached chicken breast meat can be added to this soup, if desired.

Avgolemono (pronounced ahv-go-leh-mo-no) is both a delicious classic Greek soup and a sauce made up of chicken stock, eggs and lemon juice. The sauce has less stock added so is, naturally, thicker than the soup, while the soup usually has a small amount of white rice added for texture.

avgolemono

PREPARATION TIME 10 MINUTES COOKING TIME 25 MINUTES

2.25 LITRES CHICKEN STOCK
100g WHITE SHORT-GRAIN RICE
3 EGGS, SEPARATED
80ml LEMON JUICE

1 Bring stock to a boil in large saucepan, add rice; cook, stirring occasionally, about 15 minutes or until rice is tender. Reduce heat to lowest possible setting.
2 Working quickly, beat egg whites in small bowl with electric mixer until soft peaks form. Add yolks; continue beating until combined. With motor operating, gradually add lemon juice and 250ml of the hot stock, beating until combined.
3 Remove stock mixture from heat; gradually add egg mixture, stirring constantly. Serve soup immediately.

SERVES 6
PER SERVING 3.2g FAT; 179 CAL (749KJ)

A chilled soup originating in the southern province of Andalusia in Spain, gazpacho, like other peasant soups, makes clever use of the garden's overripe vegetables.

gazpacho

PREPARATION TIME 30 MINUTES (PLUS REFRIGERATION TIME)

1 LITRE TOMATO JUICE
10 MEDIUM PLUM TOMATOES (750g), CHOPPED COARSELY
2 MEDIUM RED ONIONS (340g), CHOPPED COARSELY
2 CLOVES GARLIC, QUARTERED
½ MEDIUM CUCUMBER (130g), CHOPPED COARSELY
2 TABLESPOONS SHERRY VINEGAR
1 MEDIUM RED PEPPER (200g), CHOPPED COARSELY
1 SMALL RED ONION (100g), CHOPPED FINELY, EXTRA
½ MEDIUM CUCUMBER (130g), CHOPPED FINELY, EXTRA
1 SMALL RED PEPPER (150g), CHOPPED FINELY, EXTRA
1 TABLESPOON FINELY CHOPPED FRESH DILL

1   Blend or process juice, tomato, onion, garlic, cucumber, vinegar and pepper, in batches, until puréed. Cover; refrigerate 3 hours.
2   Just before serving, divide soup among serving bowls; stir equal amounts of extra onion, extra cucumber, extra pepper and dill into each bowl.

SERVES 6
PER SERVING 0.4g FAT; 87 CAL (366KJ)

TIPS A finely chopped red chilli added to the blender or processor makes a spicier gazpacho.

▨ Red wine vinegar can be used instead of sherry vinegar.

▨ To make this soup a complete meal, add around 6 tablespoons each of finely chopped raw celery and finely chopped green pepper to the soup, then top each serving with 1 tablespoon of finely diced hard-boiled egg and a few croutons.

vegetable soups

TIP Locally made goat's milk cheese can be substituted for the blue cheese.

broccoli &
blue cheese soup

PREPARATION TIME 15 MINUTES   COOKING TIME 30 MINUTES

1 TABLESPOON OLIVE OIL
1 LARGE ONION (200g), CHOPPED COARSELY
2 MEDIUM POTATOES (400g), CHOPPED COARSELY
500g BROCCOLI, TRIMMED, CHOPPED
2 LITRES CHICKEN STOCK
125ml DOUBLE CREAM
150g MILD BLUE CHEESE, CRUMBLED

1 Heat oil in large saucepan; cook onion, stirring, until soft. Add potato and broccoli; cook, stirring, 2 minutes.
2 Add stock, bring to a boil; simmer, uncovered, about 15 minutes or until potato is tender.
3 Blend or process soup mixture, in batches, until puréed.
4 Return soup to same cleaned pan with cream and half of the cheese; stir over heat until hot. Divide soup among serving bowls; sprinkle with remaining cheese.

SERVES 6
PER SERVING 21g FAT; 338 CAL (1415KJ)

BLUE CHEESES These are mould-treated cheeses mottled with blue veining. Varieties include firm but crumbly Stilton types to mild, creamy cheeses such as blue brie or gorgonzola.

TIPS Pushing the soup through a food mill or a sieve after the initial blending or processing results in an almost velvety-smooth texture.

You can use butternut squash instead of pumpkin.

pumpkin soup

PREPARATION TIME 20 MINUTES   COOKING TIME 35 MINUTES

40g BUTTER
1 LARGE ONION (200g), CHOPPED COARSELY
1.5kg PUMPKIN, CHOPPED COARSELY
2 LARGE POTATOES (600g), CHOPPED COARSELY
1.5 LITRES CHICKEN STOCK
125ml DOUBLE CREAM
3 TEASPOONS FINELY CHOPPED CHIVES, TO SERVE

1   Melt butter in large saucepan; cook onion, stirring, until soft. Stir in pumpkin and potato; cook, stirring, 5 minutes.
2   Stir in stock, bring to a boil; simmer, uncovered, about 20 minutes or until pumpkin is soft, stirring occasionally.
3   Blend or process soup, in batches, until puréed; push through food mill or large sieve into large clean saucepan.
4   Just before serving, add cream; stir over heat until soup is hot. Serve topped with a dollop of soured cream and a few chives, if desired.

SERVES 6
PER SERVING 14.8g FAT; 321 CAL (1346KJ)

vegetable soups

classic minestrone

100g DRIED CANNELLINI BEANS
2 TEASPOONS OLIVE OIL
1 MEDIUM ONION (150g),
CHOPPED FINELY
2 CLOVES GARLIC, CRUSHED
10 SLICES PROSCIUTTO (150g),
CHOPPED COARSELY
1 TRIMMED CELERY STICK (75g),
CHOPPED FINELY
1 MEDIUM CARROT (120g),
CHOPPED FINELY
1 MEDIUM GREEN COURGETTE
(120g), CHOPPED FINELY
2 X 400g CANS TOMATOES
1.5 LITRES CHICKEN OR VEGETABLE
STOCK
1 MEDIUM POTATO (200g), CHOPPED
FINELY
170g SOUP PASTA (SEE PAGE 62)
80g FINELY SHREDDED SAVOY
CABBAGE (SEE PAGE 24)
100g FINELY SHREDDED SPINACH
1 TABLESPOON FINELY SHREDDED
FRESH BASIL LEAVES
40g FINELY GRATED PARMESAN

There are almost as many versions of minestrone as there are Italian families, but this classic recipe is typical of those made in the north, where the colder winters require hearty fare like this. If you haven't got time to make the classic version, try our speedy alternative.

PREPARATION TIME 25 MINUTES (PLUS SOAKING TIME)
COOKING TIME 1 HOUR 10 MINUTES

1 Place beans in medium bowl, cover with water; stand overnight, drain.
2 Heat oil in large saucepan; cook onion and garlic, stirring, until onion is soft. Add prosciutto, celery, carrot and courgette; cook, stirring, 5 minutes. Stir in undrained crushed tomatoes and stock. Bring to a boil; simmer, uncovered, 30 minutes.
3 Stir in beans and potato; simmer, uncovered, 15 minutes.
4 Add pasta; simmer, uncovered, about 10 minutes or until pasta is tender.
5 Just before serving, stir in cabbage, spinach and basil; serve soup with a separate bowl of the cheese.

SERVES 6
PER SERVING 8.7g FAT; 352 CAL (1472KJ)

speedy minestrone

PREPARATION TIME 10 MINUTES   **COOKING TIME** 40 MINUTES

30g BUTTER
1 ONION (150g), SLICED THINLY
1 CLOVE GARLIC, CRUSHED
2 BACON RASHERS (140g), CHOPPED COARSELY
1 TRIMMED CELERY STALK (100g), CHOPPED COARSELY
1 MEDIUM CARROT (120g), CHOPPED COARSELY
400g CAN CHOPPED TOMATOES
310g CAN RED KIDNEY BEANS, RINSED, DRAINED
750ml CHICKEN OR VEGETABLE STOCK
120g SPIRAL PASTA
20g FLAKED PARMESAN
2 TABLESPOONS FINELY CHOPPED FRESH FLAT-LEAF PARSLEY

1 Heat butter in large saucepan, add onion, garlic and bacon; stir over medium heat until onion is soft. Add celery and carrot; stir over heat 2 minutes.
2 Stir in undrained tomatoes, beans, stock and pasta. Bring to a boil, reduce heat; simmer, covered, 30 minutes. Serve topped with cheese and parsley.

SERVES 6
PER SERVING 7.9g FAT; 180 CAL (752KJ)

TIPS Leftover steamed and chopped vegetables or boiled short pasta can be used in the soup, however, they should only be added just before serving.
■ Top each bowl of soup with a teaspoon of basil pesto, to make minestrone genovese.

TIP Recipe can be made
1 day ahead up to the end
of step 3 and refrigerated,
covered.

carrot & lentil soup
with caraway toast

1.125 LITRES VEGETABLE STOCK
2 LARGE ONIONS (400g), DICED
4 CLOVES GARLIC, CRUSHED
1 TABLESPOON GROUND CUMIN
6 LARGE CARROTS (1kg), CHOPPED
COARSELY
2 TRIMMED STICKS CELERY (150g),
CHOPPED COARSELY
500ml WATER
100g BROWN LENTILS
125ml BUTTERMILK

CARAWAY TOAST
8 SLICES (200g) CIABATTA BREAD
25g FINELY GRATED PARMESAN
CHEESE
1 TEASPOON CARAWAY SEEDS
2 TABLESPOONS FINELY CHOPPED
FRESH PARSLEY

PREPARATION TIME 25 MINUTES COOKING TIME 55 MINUTES

1 Heat 125ml stock in large saucepan; cook onion, half of the
garlic and cumin, stirring, until onion softens. Add carrot and celery;
cook, stirring, 5 minutes.
2 Add remaining stock and the water; bring to a boil. Reduce
heat; simmer, uncovered, about 20 minutes or until carrot softens.
3 Blend or process soup, in batches, until smooth; return to pan.
Add lentils; simmer, uncovered, about 20 minutes or until lentils
are tender.
4 Stir buttermilk into hot soup and serve with caraway toast.

CARAWAY TOAST Place ciabatta, in single layer, on oven tray; toast
under hot grill until browned. Sprinkle combined cheese, remaining
garlic, seeds and parsley over untoasted sides of ciabatta. Grill until
topping is browned lightly and cheese melts; cut in half.

SERVES 4
PER SERVING 4.5g FAT; 342 CAL (1433KJ)

vegetable soups

lentil & caramelised onion soup

PREPARATION TIME 10 MINUTES   COOKING TIME 25 MINUTES

400g RED LENTILS
100g BROWN RICE
1 LITRE VEGETABLE STOCK
1 LITRE WATER
1 TABLESPOON GROUND CUMIN
40g BUTTER
3 MEDIUM ONIONS (450g), SLICED THINLY
2 TABLESPOONS SUGAR
1 TABLESPOON BALSAMIC VINEGAR
PINCH CAYENNE PEPPER
4 TABLESPOONS COARSELY CHOPPED FRESH CORIANDER
4 TABLESPOONS COARSELY CHOPPED FRESH FLAT-LEAF PARSLEY
250ml VEGETABLE STOCK, EXTRA

1   Rinse lentils and rice under cold water; drain.
2   Combine stock and the water in large saucepan; bring to a boil. Add lentils, rice and cumin; return to a boil. Reduce heat; simmer, uncovered, stirring occasionally, about 15 minutes or until lentils and rice are just tender.
3   Meanwhile, melt butter in large frying pan; cook onion, stirring, until onion softens. Add sugar and vinegar; cook, stirring, until the onion caramelises.
4   Stir pepper, coriander and parsley into lentil mixture; bring to a boil. Stir in caramelised onion and extra stock; cook, stirring, until heated through.

SERVES 4
PER SERVING 12.2g FAT; 515 CAL (2153KJ)

butternut squash & aubergine laksa

PREPARATION TIME 45 MINUTES
COOKING TIME 20 MINUTES

700g PIECE BUTTERNUT SQUASH, DICED INTO 2cm PIECES
5 BABY AUBERGINES (300g), SLICED THICKLY
750ml VEGETABLE STOCK
400ml COCONUT MILK
250g RICE STICK NOODLES
500g PAK CHOY, CHOPPED COARSELY
2 TABLESPOONS LIME JUICE
100g BEANSPROUTS
6 SPRING ONIONS, SLICED THINLY
6 TABLESPOONS FRESH CORIANDER LEAVES
6 TABLESPOONS FRESH MINT LEAVES

LAKSA PASTE

7 MEDIUM DRIED RED CHILLIES
125ml BOILING WATER
1 TABLESPOON GROUNDNUT OIL
3 CLOVES GARLIC, QUARTERED
1 MEDIUM ONION (150g), CHOPPED COARSELY
10cm STICK (20g) FINELY CHOPPED FRESH LEMONGRASS
4cm PIECE FRESH GINGER (20g), GRATED
1 TABLESPOON HALVED MACADAMIAS (10g)
ROOTS FROM 1 BUNCH FRESH CORIANDER, WASHED, CHOPPED COARSELY
1 TEASPOON GROUND TURMERIC
1 TEASPOON GROUND CORIANDER
2 TEASPOONS SALT
3 TABLESPOONS FRESH MINT LEAVES

1 Make laksa paste.
2 Place 150g of the laksa paste in large saucepan; cook, stirring, about 1 minute or until fragrant. Add squash and aubergine; cook, stirring, 2 minutes. Add stock and coconut milk; bring to a boil. Reduce heat; simmer laksa mixture, covered, about 10 minutes or until vegetables are just tender.
3 Meanwhile, place noodles in large heatproof bowl, cover with boiling water, stand until just tender; drain.
4 Stir pak choy into laksa; return to a boil. Stir juice into laksa off the heat. Divide noodles among serving bowls; ladle laksa over noodles, sprinkle with combined beansprouts, onion and herbs.

LAKSA PASTE Cover chillies with the boiling water in small heatproof bowl, stand 10 minutes; drain. Blend or process chillies with remaining ingredients until mixture forms a smooth paste. Reserve 150g of the paste for this recipe; freeze remaining paste, covered, for future use.

SERVES 6
PER SERVING 20.2g FAT; 389 CAL (1626KJ)

BUTTERNUT SQUASH contains no fat, is low in kilojoules and rich in beta-carotene and vitamin C. A variety of the gramma family, the butternut has an elongated bell shape, a sweet, nutty flavour and a fairly dry texture. It is very popular and versatile. It can star as an ingredient in a soup, risotto or warm salad, and it's fab mashed then eaten on its own or made into gnocchi, a sweet pie, scones or bread.

stracciatella

PREPARATION TIME 5 MINUTES   COOKING TIME 10 MINUTES

5 EGGS
40g FINELY GRATED PARMESAN
CHEESE
1.5 LITRES CHICKEN STOCK
2 TABLESPOONS FINELY CHOPPED
FRESH FLAT-LEAF PARSLEY
PINCH NUTMEG

1   Lightly whisk eggs with cheese in medium jug until combined.
2   Bring stock to a boil in large saucepan. Remove from heat;
gradually add egg mixture, whisking constantly.
3   Return mixture to heat; simmer, stirring constantly, about
5 minutes or until egg mixture forms fine shreds. Stir in parsley
and nutmeg.
4   Serve as perfect 'comfort' food – accompanied only by a loaf
of ciabatta.

SERVES 6
PER SERVING 6.9g FAT; 145 CAL (606KJ)

Stracciatella, when translated
from Italian to English, means
strings or torn rags. This satisfying soup is thus aptly named,
since this is what the parmesan
and egg mixture resembles once
it meets the hot stock.

TIPS Break the eggs one
at a time into a small cup
before adding together in
the bowl; this way, if one egg
is stale, you can discard it.
■ Make sure you add the
egg and cheese mixture
gradually or you will end
up with large clumps of
'scrambled' egg.

TIP Any kind of bread can be used for croutons; – the ultimate garnish for soup. Rye or whole grain bread are tasty possibilities.

mushroom soup
with garlic croutons

PREPARATION TIME 20 MINUTES   COOKING TIME 40 MINUTES

250g PIECE CIABATTA BREAD
60ml OLIVE OIL
3 CLOVES GARLIC, CRUSHED
1 TABLESPOON OLIVE OIL, EXTRA
1 MEDIUM ONION (150g), CHOPPED
COARSELY
1 CLOVE GARLIC CRUSHED, EXTRA
500g CHESTNUT MUSHROOMS,
HALVED
2 LITRES BEEF OR VEGETABLE STOCK
125ml DRY WHITE WINE
1 LITRE WATER
250ml DOUBLE CREAM
1 TABLESPOON COARSELY
CHOPPED FRESH TARRAGON
LEAVES

1   Preheat oven to moderately hot. Cut bread into 2cm cubes; combine with oil and garlic in large bowl, mix well. Place bread in single layer on oven tray; toast, uncovered, stirring occasionally, in moderately hot oven about 20 minutes or until browned lightly and crisp.
2   Heat extra oil in large saucepan; cook onion and extra garlic, stirring, until onion softens. Add mushrooms; cook, stirring, about 5 minutes or until browned lightly. Stir in stock, wine and the water. Bring to a boil; simmer, uncovered, 30 minutes.
3   Blend or process soup mixture, in batches, until smooth.
4   Return soup with cream and tarragon to same cleaned pan; stir over heat until hot. Divide soup among serving bowls; top each with garlic croutons.

SERVES 6
PER SERVING 32g FAT; 458 CAL (1916KJ)

vegetable soups

curry & lime lentil soup

PREPARATION TIME 15 MINUTES
COOKING TIME 30 MINUTES

2 TEASPOONS VEGETABLE OIL
I TABLESPOON HOT CURRY PASTE
I MEDIUM ONION (150g), CHOPPED FINELY
2 CLOVES GARLIC, CRUSHED
2cm PIECE FRESH GINGER (10g), GRATED
I TEASPOON CUMIN SEEDS
200g RED LENTILS
500ml VEGETABLE STOCK
625ml WATER
400g PLUM TOMATOES, PEELED, DESEEDED AND DICED
I TEASPOON FINELY GRATED LIME RIND
60ml LIME JUICE
4 TABLESPOONS FINELY CHOPPED FRESH FLAT-LEAF PARSLEY

1   Heat oil in large saucepan; cook curry paste, stirring, until fragrant. Add onion, garlic, ginger and cumin; cook, stirring, until onion softens.
2   Add lentils, stock, the water and undrained tomatoes. Bring to a boil; reduce heat. Simmer, uncovered, about 20 minutes or until lentils are softened.
3   Stir in rind and juice; return to a boil. Remove from heat; stir in parsley.

SERVES 4
PER SERVING 6g FAT; 237 CAL (991KJ)

HOW TO PEEL TOMATOES

1   Remove the woody core at the top of each tomato.

2   Cover tomatoes with boiling water in a heatproof bowl.

3   When skin wrinkles, peel away from the core to the base.

4   Using sharp knife, pull away and discard all the tomato skin.

glossary

ALLSPICE also known as pimento or jamaican pepper; available whole or ground.

BAMBOO SHOOTS tender shoots of bamboo plants, available in cans; must be drained and rinsed before use.

BASIL aromatic herb; there are many types, but the most commonly used is sweet basil.

BAY LEAVES aromatic leaves from the bay tree available fresh or dried; used to add a strong, slightly peppery flavour to soups, stocks and casseroles.

BEANS

black also known as turtle beans or black kidney beans, they are an earthy-flavoured dried bean different from the better-known Chinese black beans (which are fermented soy beans).

black-eye also known as black-eyed peas; small beige legumes with black circular eyes. Available dried or tinned.

cannellini small, dried white bean similar to other *Phaseolus vulgaris* (great northern, navy and haricot beans).

red kidney pink to maroon beans with a floury texture and fairly sweet flavour; sold dried or tinned.

BEANSPROUTS also known as bean shoots; tender new growths of assorted beans and seeds germinated for consumption as sprouts.

BICARBONATE OF SODA also called baking soda.

BUTTERMILK fresh low-fat milk cultured to give a slightly sour, tangy taste; low-fat yogurt or milk can be substituted.

BUTTERNUT SQUASH sometimes used interchangeably with the word pumpkin, butternut squash is a member of the gourd family.

CALAMARI a mollusc, a type of squid; substitute with baby octopus.

CARAWAY SEEDS a member of the parsley family; available in seed or ground form.

CARDAMOM can be bought in pod, seed or ground form. Has a distinctive, aromatic, sweetly rich flavour.

CAYENNE PEPPER thin-fleshed, long, very-hot red chilli; usually purchased dried and ground.

CHEESE

cheddar the most common cow's milk 'tasty' cheese; should be aged and hard.

gruyere a firm, cow's milk Swiss cheese having small holes and a nutty, slightly salty flavour. Emmental or appenzeller can be used as a substitute.

parmesan sharp-tasting, dry, hard cheese, made from skimmed or semi-skimmed milk and aged for at least a year.

CHERVIL also known as cicily; mildly fennel-flavoured herb with curly dark-green leaves.

CHICKPEAS also called garbanzos, hummus or channa; an irregularly round, sandy-coloured legume.

CHILLIES available in many types and sizes, both fresh and dried. The smaller the chilli, the hotter it is. Wear rubber gloves when handling chillies, as they can burn your skin. Removing seeds and membranes lessens the heat level.

thai small, medium hot, and bright-red to dark-green in colour.

CHIVES related to the onion and leek, with subtle onion flavour.

CHORIZO a sausage of Spanish origin; made of coarsely ground pork and seasoned with garlic and chillies.

CIABATTA meaning 'slipper' in Italian, the traditional shape of this popular crisp-crusted white bread.

CINNAMON dried inner bark of the shoots of the cinnamon tree.

CLAMS also known as vongole; we use a small ridge-shelled variety of this bivalve mollusc.

CLOVES can be used whole or in ground form. Has a strong scent and taste so should be used minimally.

COCONUT MILK unsweetened coconut milk available in cans.

CORIANDER

dried a fragrant herb; seeds and ground coriander must never be used in place of fresh coriander or vice versa. The tastes are completely different.

fresh also known as cilantro or chinese parsley; bright-green-leafed herb with a pungent flavour.

CRÈME FRAÎCHE a mature fermented cream (minimum fat content 35%) having a slightly tangy flavour and velvety rich texture; similar thickness to soured cream.

CUMIN available both ground and as whole seeds; cumin has a warm, earthy, rather strong flavour.

CURRY POWDER a blend of ground spices; choose mild or hot to suit your taste and the recipe.

FISH SAUCE also called nam pla or nuoc nam; made from pulverised salted fermented fish, mostly anchovies. Has a pungent smell and strong taste; use sparingly.

EVAPORATED MILK we used canned milk with 1.6g fat per 100ml.

FLAT-LEAF PARSLEY also known as continental parsley or italian parsley.

FLOUR

plain all-purpose flour.

self-raising plain flour sifted with baking powder (a raising agent consisting mainly of 2 parts cream of tartar to 1 part bicarbonate of soda) in the proportion of 150g flour to 2 level teaspoons baking powder.

GALANGAL also known as laos; a dried root that is a member of the ginger family, used whole or ground, having a piquant, peppery flavour.

GINGER also called green or root ginger; the thick gnarled root of a tropical plant. Can be kept, peeled, covered with dry sherry in a jar and refrigerated, or frozen in an airtight container.

HERBS we have specified when to use fresh or dried herbs. Use dried (not ground) herbs in the proportions of 1:4 for fresh herbs, for example 1 teaspoon dried herbs instead of 4 teaspoons chopped fresh herbs.

KAFFIR LIME LEAVES aromatic leaves used fresh or dried in Asian dishes.

KECAP MANIS an Indonesian sweet, thick soy sauce which has sugar and spices added.

LAKSA bottled paste of lemongrass, chillies, onions, galangal, shrimp paste and turmeric used to make the classic soup by the same name.

LEMONGRASS a tall, clumping, lemon-smelling and tasting, sharp edged grass; use only the white lower part of each stem.

LENTILS many varieties of dried legumes, identified by and named after their colour.

MACADAMIAS native to Australia, a rich and buttery nut; store in refrigerator because of its high oil content.

MUSHROOMS

chestnut light to dark brown mushrooms with mild, earthy flavour.

shiitake cultivated fresh mushroom; has a rich, meaty flavour.

MUSSELS must be tightly closed when bought, indicating they are alive. Before cooking, scrub shells with a strong brush and remove 'beards'. Discard any that do not open after cooking.

NOODLES

beanthread also known as cellophane or glass noodles, or bean thread vermicelli.

rice stick especially popular South East Asian dried rice noodles. They come in different widths, but all should be soaked in hot water to soften.

singapore Pre-cooked wheat noodles best described as a thinner version of hokkien; sold, packaged, in the refrigerated section of supermarkets.

NUTMEG dried nut of an evergreen tree; available in ground form or you can grate your own with a fine grater.

OIL

groundnut pressed from ground peanuts. Commonly used in stir-frying because of its high smoke point.

olive mono-unsaturated; made from the pressing of tree-ripened olives. Extra virgin and virgin are the best, obtained from the first pressings of the olive, while extra light or light refers to the taste, not fat levels.

sesame made from roasted, crushed, white sesame seeds; a flavouring rather than a cooking medium.

vegetable any number of oils sourced from plants rather than animal fats.

OKRA also known as gumbo or lady's fingers; a green, ridged, oblong pod with a furry skin used to thicken stews. Rinse and cut off capped end close to stalk.

OYSTERS a bivalve mollusc; when buying, look for oysters that are plump and glossy and smell fresh.

PAK CHOY also called bok choi or Chinese chard; has a mild mustard taste and is good braised or in stir-fries. Baby pak choy is also available.

PALM SUGAR made from the sap of the sugar palm tree. Light brown to black in colour; usually sold in rock-hard cakes. If unavailable, use brown sugar. Available from some supermarkets and Asian food stores.

PAPRIKA ground dried red bell pepper (capsicum); available sweet or hot. pastrami spicy smoked beef, ready to eat when bought.

PEARL BARLEY the husk is removed, then hulled and polished so that the 'pearl' of the original grain remains, much the same as white rice.

PEPPERCORNS available in black, white, red or green.

sichuan also known as szechuan or chinese pepper. Small, reddish-brown berries with distinctive peppery-lemon flavour and aroma.

PINE NUTS also known as pignoli; small, cream-coloured kernels obtained from the cones of different varieties of pine trees.

PITTA BREAD a lightly leavened, soft, flat bread. When baked, the bread puffs up, leaving a pocket, which can be stuffed with savoury fillings. Pitta is also eaten with dips or soups.

POLENTA a flour-like cereal made of ground corn; similar to cornmeal but finer and lighter in colour; also the name of the dish made from it.

PROSCIUTTO salted-cured, air-dried (unsmoked), pressed ham; usually sold in paper-thin slices, ready to eat.

RICE

brown natural whole grain.

jasmine sometimes sold as Thai fragrant rice, Jasmine rice is so-named due to its sweet aroma.

long grain elongated grain, remains separate when cooked; most popular steaming rice in Asia.

SAFFRON one of the most expensive spices in the world, true saffron comes only from the saffron crocus, that produces several flowers a year.

SCALLOPS a bivalve mollusc with fluted shell valve; we use scallops having the coral (roe) attached.

SHALLOTS also called french shallots, golden shallots or eschalots; small, elongated, brown-skinned members of the onion family. Grows in tight clusters similar to garlic.

SHRIMP PASTE pungent, preserved, almost solid paste made of salted dried shrimp.

SOURED CREAM a thick commercially-cultured soured cream. Minimum fat content 35%.

SOY SAUCE made from fermented soy beans; several variations are available.

STAR ANISE a dried star-shaped pod; the seeds taste of aniseed.

SWEET CHILLI SAUCE mild, Thai sauce made from red chillies, sugar, garlic and vinegar.

THAI GREEN CURRY PASTE The hottest of the traditional pastes; used in chicken and vegetable curries and stir-fries and noodle dishes.

TOFU also known as bean curd, an off-white, custard-like product made from the 'milk' of crushed soy beans; comes fresh as soft or firm, and processed as fried or pressed dried sheets.

TURMERIC a member of the ginger family, its root is dried and ground; intensely pungent in taste but not hot.

VINEGAR

balsamic authentic only from the province of Modena, Italy; made from a regional wine of white trebbiano grapes specially processed then aged in antique wooden casks to give the exquisite pungent flavour.

cider made from fermented apples.

red wine based on fermented red wine.

sherry mellow wine vinegar named for its colour.

white wine based on fermented white wine.

WHOLEGRAIN MUSTARD also known as seeded. A French-style coarse-grain mustard made from crushed mustard seeds and Dijon-style French mustard.

WORCESTERSHIRE SAUCE a thin, dark-brown, spicy sauce used as seasoning for meat and gravies, and as a condiment.

index

conversion charts

WARNING This book may contain recipes for dishes made with raw or lightly cooked eggs. These should be avoided by vulnerable people such as pregnant and nursing mothers, invalids, the elderly, babies and young children.

MEASURES

■ The spoon measurements used in this book are metric: one metric tablespoon holds 20ml; one metric teaspoon holds 5ml.

■ All spoon measurements are level.

■ The most accurate way of measuring dry ingredients is to weigh them.

■ When measuring liquids, use a clear glass or plastic jug with metric markings.

■ We use large eggs with an average weight of 60g.

DRY MEASURES

metric	imperial
15g	$1/2$oz
30g	1oz
60g	2oz
90g	3oz
125g	4oz ($1/4$lb)
155g	5oz
185g	6oz
220g	7oz
250g	8oz ($1/2$lb)
280g	9oz
315g	10oz
345g	11oz
375g	12oz ($3/4$lb)
410g	13oz
440g	14oz
470g	15oz
500g	16oz (1lb)
750g	24oz (1$1/2$lb)
1kg	32oz (2lb)

LIQUID MEASURES

metric	imperial
30ml	1 fl oz
60ml	2 fl oz
100ml	3 fl oz
125ml	4 fl oz
150ml	5 fl oz ($1/4$ pint/1 gill)
190ml	6 fl oz
250ml	8 fl oz
300ml	10 fl oz ($1/2$ pt)
500ml	16 fl oz
600ml	20 fl oz (1 pint)
1000ml (1 litre)	1$3/4$ pints

LENGTH MEASURES

metric	imperial
3mm	$1/8$in
6mm	$1/4$in
1cm	$1/2$in
2cm	$3/4$in
2.5cm	1in
5cm	2in
6cm	2$1/2$in
8cm	3in
10cm	4in
13cm	5in
15cm	6in
18cm	7in
20cm	8in
23cm	9in
25cm	10in
28cm	11in
30cm	12in (1ft)

OVEN TEMPERATURES

These oven temperatures are only a guide for conventional ovens. For fan-assisted ovens, check the manufacturer's manual.

	°C (Celcius)	°F (Fahrenheit)	gas mark
Very low	120	250	$1/2$
Low	150	275-300	1-2
Moderately low	170	325	3
Moderate	180	350-375	4-5
Moderately hot	200	400	6
Hot	220	425-450	7-8
Very hot	240	475	9